P9-BYZ-766

DISCARD
Porter County
Library System

Valparaiso Public Library
103 Jefferson St.
Valparaiso, IN 46383

The Best Friend's Guide to Planning a Wedding

The Best Friend's Guide to Planning a Wedding

How to Find a Dress, Return the Shoes,

Hire a Caterer, Fire the Photographer,

Choose a Florist, Book a Band, and

Still Wind Up Married at the End of It All

LARA WEBB CARRIGAN

PORTER COUNTY PUBLIC LIBRARY SYSTEM

Valparaiso Public Library
103 Jefferson St.
Valparaiso, IN 46383

395.22 CAR   VAL
Carrigan, Lara Webb.
The best friend's guide t
planning a wedding : how
33410006243978

AUG 0 3 2001

ReganBooks

An Imprint of HarperCollinsPublishers

To Brian, my true love

and Olive, who helped me find him

THE BEST FRIEND'S GUIDE TO PLANNING A WEDDING. Copyright ©
2001 by Lara Webb Carrigan. All rights reserved. Printed in the United
States of America. No part of this book may be used or reproduced in any
manner whatsoever without written permission except in the case of brief
quotations embodied in critical articles and reviews. For information address
HarperCollins Publishers Inc., 10 East 53rd Street, New York, NY 10022.

HarperCollins books may be purchased for educational, business, or sales
promotional use. For information please write: Special Markets Department,
HarperCollins Publishers Inc., 10 East 53rd Street, New York, NY 10022.

FIRST EDITION

Design by Gretchen Achilles

Printed on acid-free paper

Library of Congress Cataloging-in-Publication Data
Carrigan, Lara Webb.
   The best friend's guide to planning a wedding : how to find a dress,
return the shoes, hire a caterer, fire the photographer, choose a florist,
book a band, and still wind up married at the end of it all / by Lara Webb
Carrigan
                          p. cm.
      ISBN 0-06-039301-7
      1. Weddings—Planning. I. Title.
   HQ745 .C39 2001
   395.2'2—dc21   00-042543

01 02 03 04 05 ❖/RRD 10 9 8 7 6 5 4 3 2 1

Contents

Introduction   ix

PART I:

Way Before
1

THE PROPOSAL: How It Happens   3

TIME TO PLAN   6

TIME TO REPLAN   7

THE PLAN: Who, What, When, Where, and Why   8

THE BUDGET: Is That Money in Your Pocket or
    Are You Just Happy to See Me?   29

AFTER THE PLAN: Your Groom and What to Do
    with Him   39

THE ATTENDANTS: Who's In, Who's Out   46

MOTHERS AND MOTHERS-IN-LAW:
    Handle with Care   58

PART II:

A Little Before

65

VOWS: Your Ceremony and You   67

CATERERS: Minding Your Ps and Qs   81

CAKE: His and Hers   92

MUSIC: Bands, DJs, and All That Jazz   97

FLOWERS: A Rose Is a Rose Is a Rose   116

PICTURES: To Shoot or Not to Shoot   126

INVITATIONS: The Name Game   140

THE DRESS: From Sample Sale to Seamstress   151

DRESSING EVERYBODY ELSE   164

PART III:

Right Before

175

REGISTERING: Eenie Meenie Minie Mo   177

PRIMPING 101: How to Make Yourself Beautiful   187

DETAILS: The Little Things That Count   199

WEDDING COUNTDOWN: Keeping Track
    of the Details   205

PART IV:

During

215

THE REHEARSAL: If at First You Don't Succeed,
Try, Try Again   217

THE REHEARSAL DINNER: Toasts, Jokes, and Other
Embarrassing Moments   221

THE CEREMONY: I Do (I Think)   225

THE RECEPTION: Where's the Party?   228

THE GETAWAY   234

PART V:

After

235

THE HONEYMOON: Going, Going, Gone   237

Acknowledgments   245

Introduction

This is an easy-to-read, fairly short book with lots of chapters, mini-chapters, headings, subheadings, a footnote, even a detailed table of contents. Because really, a wedding is an easy, fairly short thing. There just happen to be a lot of steps along the way—many seemingly complicated steps, choices, decisions, and dilemmas that could threaten your mental health. What do you do? You do what every girl has ever done since steps, choices, decisions, and dilemmas (and certainly weddings) were invented—you turn to your best friend. And in your best friend's honest, loving, and oh-so-wise way, she'll tell you: A wedding is a wacky thing. It is part ceremony, part celebration, part family reunion, part college reunion, part high school reunion, part concert, part worship service. . . . Well, you get the idea. So it's no wonder that making your wedding the best day of your life (we've all heard that line, right?) sometimes seems a little ludicrous.

And it is. It's a ludicrous, extravagant, and downright silly tradition. What's to be done about it? you ask her. Nothing. Acknowledge it from the start, laugh at it, grin, snicker, smile. Because if you laugh at the little things along the way, smile in the face of those trying times (and there will be trying times—very, very trying), maybe, just maybe, you won't wind up cackling in the nuthouse at the end of it all. And since your best friend seems to have survived her own wedding pretty much intact (except for that one weird tic she's developed whenever you mention rice), you listen, take heart, and laugh.

So that's what this book is: a guide to staying out of the nuthouse, to surviving the journey that faces every bride-to-be, and to enjoying yourself along the way. It's like your best friend—funny, informative, full of anecdotes, stories, tips, hints, and good old-fashioned yarns. This book, like every best friend, might even be a teensy bit helpful. It is *The Best Friend's Guide to Planning a Wedding.* Enjoy.

PART I

Way Before

The Proposal

HOW IT HAPPENS

The Scene: I'm at a bed and breakfast in Mystic, Connecticut. A roaring fire warms the oak-paneled floors. White-eyelet curtains flutter at the windows as a winter breeze comes blustering in. A four-poster bed stands grandly in the middle of the room with a deep, down comforter and luxurious down pillows. A dozen red and white roses are on one side of the bed. A vase of lilies, their perfume wafting through the room, is on the other. I'm sitting in a white wicker chair with a bottle of champagne and a tray of white-chocolate-dipped strawberries on a small wicker table in front of me. Brian is on one knee. He's professing his love, talking about our future, and slipping the most unbelievably beautiful diamond onto my finger. I look into his eyes, and for a split second I think:

How in the world did this happen?

Insert your own engagement scene above, and I'm sure the question occurred to you, too. But the question isn't all that easy to answer, is it?

I mean, as a child you always knew life and marriage and all that stuff would be easy. In the words of one young thinker: "Once I'm done with kindergarten, I'm going to find myself a husband." When you get older the subject still seems pretty easy: You aren't going to get married at all. You are going to climb the corporate ladder, or become an artist, or a writer. You are going to live alone with your cats (or your dog, or bird, hey, maybe even an iguana), go out to lunch with your girlfriends, and live a perfectly happy, self-sufficient life without the misery, heartache, and yuckiness that men always seem to bring along with them.

And then, something happens. Something difficult to explain to the child in you, and something even more difficult to explain to the adult in you. Something not so easy. You meet someone. At the grocery store, or a restaurant, or a dance. (Anika, for instance, found her future husband at the copy machine, which just goes to show that you never can tell about these kinds of things.) And with a shock you realize he's funnier than you expected. Nicer, too. He listens, and actually discovers parts of you that you didn't even know existed. And for some off-the-wall reason he doesn't think your habit of staring at walls (or craving broccoli at 2 A.M., or singing old nursery rhymes when you're nervous) is really all that weird.

But now that you're completely happy—happier than you ever imagined—you're also a bit confused. If *you're* not weird (and you are, too, you insist), *he* must be. How can he possibly think I'm normal, desirable, or interesting? you ask. How can he possibly want to date me? And however in the world can he say he *loves* me? *He* must be the weird one. After all, he has that funny habit of picking at his feet. He likes to eat his toast burnt. He leaves gum in little dried-up wads all over the apartment. The list grows. And if you're like me, you come to the only conclusion one can under such circumstances: You have to break up with him. Or, you play a ridiculous game of chicken, sending out unbearably mixed signals until *he* is forced to break up with *you*.

Then something a little more difficult happens. You miss him. You miss his feet and his burnt toast. Part of you even misses his chewing gum. After all, he's nice. He's funny. And all of a sudden you feel horrible, because all of a sudden you realize what you never, ever thought you could, or would: You love him. And now, you need him back. You get him, too, because for all of the stories that men are emotionally insecure, fearful of commitment, and shy of the word "love," there are just as many stories where the women turn out to be timid, weak, and even a little bit stupid. In these stories it's the men who wait for the women. Brian did. He listened as I tearfully explained all the things I had never been able to say before about commitment and broccoli and gum and those rhymes and, well, about how I loved him. And after a few tears of his own, we were, sigh, together again, and together, we started to think about the future, until one blustery Friday I was being whisked away from work through the New England countryside to a quaint little bed and breakfast in Mystic.

Oh, I think, so that's how I got here. And looking into his big, brown eyes, with reflections of me and only me, I say yes. Yes, yes, yes.

What happens next? Who cares? You eat, you drink, you walk around together. You smile a lot. Kiss a lot. Hold hands a lot. You're engaged. Nothing else matters.

Time to Plan

This occurs approximately an hour or two after the proposal, while you're still on that nice, I'm-engaged-now high. You will have a very fun, enjoyable, even relaxed time dreaming up sites for your reception, naming favorite wines you've had that you should serve (the wine you're drinking now, for instance), and deciding which best friends will be in your wedding party. In fact, everything about your wedding plan at this point is about exactly that: the wedding *party*. None of that stuffy, formal stuff for you. You are going to make sure your wedding is fun. After all, you're the fun couple. All of your friends are fun. Oh, isn't life fun?

This plan will last approximately one to two hours, at which point it will be time to replan. See the next chapter.

Time to Replan

This occurs once you have stopped drinking that fabulous wine and are sitting down with a pen and paper. You start the guest list and realize you're not sure if you're supposed to invite all of your relatives from Kentucky or just the ones you've met before. And what about your new stepmother's side of the family? What's the etiquette? Do you invite your new friend from your new job and, if you do, do you have to invite your new boss? If he invites his boss, does he have to invite the whole office? And then there's the seemingly simple task of choosing your wedding party. Except for the fact that it's not that simple: He has four best friends, three brothers, and a sister. You have seven best friends, a sister, and a cousin. Wait, you suddenly say, shouldn't there be a book on this? You scrap the plan and go back to having fun. The real plan can come later.

The Plan

WHO, WHAT, WHEN, WHERE, AND WHY

Jennifer used a blue three-ring binder to organize her wedding plan. She carefully divided the notebook into separate sections for each vendor, labeling each section with a different-colored tab and obsessively making sure each contract, receipt, and piece of correspondence was in its proper place. She made herself a to-do list every day and checked each task off dutifully as she completed it.

Jill was equally organized but used a specially designed wedding software program. With the click of a button, she could pull up her guest list to see who was coming, who wasn't, who had sent a gift, who hadn't, and even cross-reference a specific guest's name to see what time their plane was arriving, who in the family had a dietary restriction, and if they needed a baby-sitter for Friday night, Saturday night, or both.

Now, three-ring binders and wedding software programs can be helpful (Katherine, a particularly tech-savvy bride-to-be, swears by her Palm Pilot). On the other hand, you may be a Post-it Note to the refrigerator, the phone, the bathroom mirror, even the front door kind of girl (this is roughly the method I used). But know that while fancy planners and even fancier technology may not be absolutely necessary, having a plan absolutely is. As romantic and magical as your engagement may have been, weddings do not just magically happen. Weddings take work. And whether you, your mother, his mother, or a hired consultant will be doing the work, somebody is going to need a plan to ensure that, amid all the details, excitement, hoopla, and traumas that are about to commence, you and your groom-to-be somehow wind up married (smiling, laughing, and still completely in love) at the end of it all.

So how do I come up with a plan? The following chapter should help, providing you and your groom—perhaps even your families—with the opportunity to discuss each person's visions of the ceremony, the reception, the flowers, the dress, the, well, you'll see. This is also your chance to throw up your hands and run off to Vegas (it's not too late now, but it might be later). *Sounds easy enough. Will I need anything else?* Lots of pens, lots of paper, and lots of patience. This could take awhile.

WHO

Ask yourself who you are holding your wedding for. If you've always thought of a wedding as an intimate and personal exchange of vows between two people, you might choose to plan a private ceremony for just the two of you. Aleena and Joseph, for example, a couple both marrying for the second time, had long outgrown dreams of a fairy-tale wedding, but felt their love and marriage were no less real the second time around. With one phone call, they were able to arrange a private ceremony on a beach in the Bahamas. The champagne, cake, flowers, minister, even two witnesses were included. "An hour before we exchanged vows we were swimming in the pool. An hour after the ceremony we were back in the pool watching a trapeze instructor teach guests how to swing into the water. On the one hand, it was completely silly and spontaneous. On the other hand, it was simple and special. We're not kids anymore, but our wedding made us feel like kids again."

Another couple, tired of the grand, spectator-sport-like weddings they had attended in the past, chose a private but no less exciting option: One afternoon after washing Tom's car, he and Cindy drove two blocks to a drive-thru wedding chapel that had recently opened in their small Florida town. With balloons and streamers dancing around them and organ music playing over a speaker, they said their vows, and minutes later were back in Tom's driveway. "We had had our marriage license for a while, but just couldn't seem to make it to the courthouse," Tom said. "We wanted to do something simple but fun. The drive-thru was perfect: quick and easy—plus, they even threw in a free bottle of champagne."

However, your wedding dream may include more people than just you and your groom. Linda and Mitch had been dating for almost ten years when they decided to finally tie the knot. They were hoping to run down to city hall for a quick, private ceremony but knew their families would never forgive them. In the end, they invited twenty-five friends and family to join them at city hall and then slipped out of town for a private honeymoon.

My sister's wedding was also purposefully small. She and her groom-to-be were graduating from college and had immediate plans to move to San Francisco. Planning a large wedding in the middle of exams and final papers would have been impossible, and unnecessary, they decided. "Having a few friends and just our closest family members surround us on our wedding day felt exactly right." The morning of their wedding everybody gathered by the river while Shelley came floating down the path with our dad in a simple, vintage dress. Afterward, we toasted the lucky couple over a casual buffet brunch and then waved good-bye as they headed off on their two-week drive to San Francisco. Everything was small but perfect, and I, needless to say, cried my eyes out.

> *Wedding Myth* #1: **The more people you invite to your wedding, the more fun it will be.** *The more people you invite to your wedding, the more people you are going to have to eat with, drink with, dance with, toast to, talk to, and toss your bouquet to—all in approximately four hours. You be the judge.*

But for many brides, a wedding just wouldn't be a wedding without all of their college friends, high school friends, childhood friends, and family, no matter how near or far. By the time Brian and I said "I do," we had been dating for almost five years. We saw our wedding as a once-in-a-lifetime opportunity to celebrate both our own love (and that ecstatic moment where we joined our lives together forever and ever) and the love we had for all of our friends and families who had supported us over the years (and who were probably just as ecstatic to see us get hitched and get on with it already). Our wedding, then, was to be a madcap celebration of marriage, love, and tradition, and as we sat down to make our wedding plan, we made sure each decision we made reflected all three.

Once you've decided who the wedding will be for, here's another tricky question: *Who* will be planning the wedding? If your wedding and reception are for your families and friends, your family and his family (and perhaps even a friend or two) may want to offer their input, especially if they are helping to pay for the event. If their help is welcome, feel free to delegate. Put your groom in charge of hiring a band, your mother in charge of reserving the synagogue and rabbi, and his mother in charge of planning the rehearsal dinner or kiddush. And if there are any other family members willing to pitch in, by all means put them to work.

However, if you're worried that your families' wedding plans will bear little (if any) resemblance to your own wedding plans, now is the time to say so. Planning a wedding requires honesty. It also requires tact and respect. If you and your fiancé are accepting your families' financial help, you will also need to respect their right to help with the planning—or at least to offer their opinions. But if your families' opinions come across more like demands, it may mean enough to you and your groom-to-be to foot the bill yourselves. Compromise can be a complicated thing, but it's not impossible. This is your dream, but it's not just your day. If you can make your mother happy simply by tucking a piece of lace in your hair, by all means, indulge her. And if dancing with your father to Frank Sinatra would make him the proudest pop on the face of the earth, I'm sure you'll find it hard to say no. By listening to others' wishes and visions for the wedding day—and honoring those you know are most important—you'll ensure that everybody listens and honors your dream, too.

WHAT

Deciding what kind of wedding to have may be the most enjoyable part of the whole wedding process. Feel free to explore traditional wedding ceremonies and receptions as well as not-so-traditional options. Just because you and your future groom are running off to Mexico for a dual wedding and honeymoon doesn't mean you can't return home and throw a huge party for all of your friends and family. And holding a ceremony for family members only doesn't mean you'll need to have a casual wedding by the river or a quiet ceremony in your church's chapel. Instead, you might rent out the private room of an expensive restaurant and treat your families to an elegant seven-course meal. Tracey and Bob, for instance, held their family wedding on Bob's father's yacht and returned to shore just as the sun was setting for chilled champagne and baked clams. "I remember the stars were so bright that night and Bob and I just kept staring at them, completely in awe of the new life we were about to start together, but also completely surrounded by family who supported us. I will never forget that feeling."

Like Tracey and Bob, you and your fiancé will want to consider what you want your wedding to feel like—intimate, elegant, formal, festive, casual, fun, spiritual, romantic? What are your personalities? What kind of atmosphere do you want to create for your guests? What ethnic or religious traditions would you like to honor? Make a list of adjectives that describe how you want to feel on your wedding day, and as you start creating your wedding plan (choosing reception sites, hiring a band), think of ways to reflect the characteristics most important to you.

So what are your options? These days the only rule about what kinds of weddings are acceptable is that there are no rules. Brides and grooms are getting married on horseback, on surfboards, underwater, while skydiving, riding in hot-air balloons, and bungee jumping. This is what I like to call the extreme sports genre of weddings, and while the sky seems to be the limit thus far (there haven't been any marriages in space that I'm aware of), most of these weddings are confined only by the couple's imagination.

However, some couples may be a bit more timid. And even the two rock climbers exchanging vows may eventually want to return to the ground to celebrate with their friends and family. Some traditional wedding options include a wedding breakfast/brunch, wedding lunch, wedding tea, wedding cocktail party, wedding dessert party, or wedding dinner party. It's also not unheard of to combine different types of weddings. Many dinner parties begin with a cocktail hour, while some wedding celebrations are all-day affairs, with a morning ceremony followed by a light lunch and then a dinner party later in the evening complete with drinking and dancing.

The kind of wedding you decide to have will also determine what other events will be surrounding it. If you plan on throwing a lavish dinner party for friends and family from all over, you might need to plan a dinner the evening before the wedding for your wedding party and out-of-town guests. Many grooms' parents volunteer to host this function (sometimes called the rehearsal dinner), since traditionally the wedding is held in the bride's hometown and most of the out-of-town guests are on the groom's side. On the other hand, some brides' families choose to host a dinner at their home or country club. You and your groom may want to take charge of the event yourselves and rent out a room in your favorite restaurant or bar.

Your wedding might also include other activities such as a golf outing, a bridesmaids' luncheon, a brunch thrown the morning of the wedding, and perhaps even another one the morning after. Sarita, a Hindu bride, planned a party for all her female guests the evening before her wedding with traditional Pakistani music and dancing and a henna artist who decorated the women's hands and feet with the traditional thick auburn ink used in this prewedding ritual. But whatever events you decide to have, keep in mind that you will need to add them to your wedding plan, making sure that you have enough time—and enough people—to coordinate each event.

WHEN

Deciding when to hold your wedding means deciding on a number of variables: the season, year, time of day, month, and day of the week. Some brides have even been known to take into account planetary alignment. However, for many brides, trying to figure out the exact second to start their ceremony would be a little like planning a heart attack. Let's start with the season instead.

SEASON Picking a season largely means picking your weather. If you've always dreamed of an outdoor, mountaintop ceremony with crisp breezes and dozens of red, orange, and yellow leaves falling all around you, then no season but fall will do. On the other hand, if you've always envisioned pulling away from your reception in a horse-drawn sleigh with dozens of snowflakes falling all around, then you'll want to plan a winter wedding. Certain seasons might also remind you of when you and your groom-to-be first met. Susan and John met on a softball team, and the smell of cut grass, dirt, and bubble gum still conjures up their first summer of love. They exchanged vows on an exquisitely hot summer day right on the pitcher's mound, followed by a reception in the air-conditioned clubhouse, complete with hot dogs, hamburgers, ice-cold colas and beers, and bubble gum favors, of course.

Choosing a season may also mean taking into account work and school schedules. Michaela knew that fall was a busy time of year for both her and her future husband. Spring was a relatively calm season and allowed them plenty of time to take care of last-minute wedding details and to enjoy a much needed, two-week honeymoon in Hawaii. Also consider your friends and families: Students, teachers, and school administrators, for instance, may still be in school and will have their own academic schedules to work around.

YEAR Choosing the year of your wedding mainly means deciding how much time you feel you'll need to plan. According to most magazine checklists, the average bride takes a year to plan her wedding. Some brides, however, will need far more time, some far less. If you're the kind of person who will need to interview at least six caterers before deciding on one, give yourself plenty of time to plan. Also keep in mind that the more time you allow yourself for planning, the more time you'll have to deal with cancellations (unfortunately, this does happen) and last-minute catastrophes (these happen, too).

Reserving your band and other vendors early may also mean a savings on next year's prices, as most vendors tend to raise their fees every year. Jill and Ted, for instance, were fortunate enough to contract a certain price for their favorite wine before it made the cover of *Wine Spectator* and grew in popularity—and price.

TIME OF DAY Picking a time of day for your wedding means choosing a certain level of formality. Informal wedding ceremonies are traditionally held in the mornings, afternoons, and in the evenings up until 5:30 P.M. Wedding receptions tend to be shorter and less expensive and include lighter foods. Casual attire is acceptable. Formal ceremonies traditionally begin after 6 P.M., suggesting to guests that formal attire is required: Men wear tuxedos; women wear evening dresses. A sit-down dinner or large buffet dinner is served and is usually followed by dancing.

*Wedding Myth # 2: **Evening weddings are more fun than morning weddings.** They can be. They can also be more work to plan, more expensive, and far stuffier than morning weddings.*

However, you know the rules regarding traditions these days: They're being broken all over the place. Angie and Jeremy's ceremony, for example, started at 7 P.M. To convey to guests that the atmosphere was to be sophisticated, yet casual (no formal wear required), they sent out simple white invitations on heavy card stock with informal wording in navy ink. Danielle's wedding ceremony, on the other hand, started at 4 P.M. The Greek Orthodox ceremony was to last two hours, and the reception, beginning at seven, was to be a formal affair. She also used her invitation to convey the level of formality by having the words "black tie" engraved in the bottom-left corner.

You and your groom will also want to discuss the timing between your ceremony and reception. Some brides will want to proceed to the reception immediately after the wedding, while some will choose to have formal pictures taken after the ceremony with their families and their wedding party. This might mean a two-, or more, hour delay between the ceremony and the reception, in which guests might return to their hotels to "freshen up" or drop smaller children at a baby-sitter's. Some couples decide to host a cocktail hour for guests at the reception site while they are having photographs taken. Or consider hosting a "swing" wedding, where an instructor teaches guests how to dance at the reception site while the wedding party is out getting their pictures taken. You should also decide on times for other wedding events, including the rehearsal, rehearsal dinner, and any other activities that require making reservations.

Again, there are no real rules regulating what time of day you should hold your wedding ceremony and reception. But different times of day do generally inspire certain moods and reflect certain levels of formality. Although Tracey was able to hire her band for one third of the cost by holding an afternoon wedding, for some reason, her guests found it hard to boogie oogie oogie at noon. And while Sarah meant well by suggesting her guests would be more comfortable in casual attire at her outside tent wedding, she was appalled to find half of the male guests involved in a game of tackle football after the cutting of the cake. Before throwing traditions to the wind, remember that some of them were invented for a reason.

MONTH/DAY Deciding on the month and day for your wedding has the potential to be rather tricky and may take a bit of research. If your wedding will include family members, be sure and get a schedule of other major family events: graduations, reunions, other weddings, vacations. You may also want to check sports schedules, since one uncle of a bride I've known politely declined to attend her ceremony because his favorite football team was having a home game in the same town as the wedding. Similarly, you may want to check your friends' calendars, especially if you are asking them to be a part of your wedding ceremony. Jennifer, for example, planned her wedding around her best lady's baby's due date.

Also consider that some religions will not allow couples to marry during certain times of the year or even on certain days of the week. Although many churches have become more flexible, you will want to check with your rabbi, priest, or minister before setting a date. Make sure to take into account that other holidays, such as Christmas, New Year's Eve, and Valentine's Day, may be particularly busy times of the year for caterers and florists. For example, you might pay twice as much for a bouquet of roses the weekend of Valentine's Day as you would just one weekend later. However, if your heart is set on a Valentine's Day wedding (this is your dream, after all), talk candidly with your florist. By planning far enough in advance, she may be able to order enough bouquets for both her Valentine's Day customers and your wedding—at a reasonable price.

Also recognize that the months from June to October are the

busiest for weddings and that Saturday is the busiest day of the week. Check with your reception site for availability before setting your heart on a specific date, and ask if your reception site has any other weddings scheduled for the same day. Many wedding banquet halls and hotel ballrooms hold more than one wedding a day during the busy season and the effect can seem a bit like a wedding factory. If you are at all flexible, you may be able to reserve your reception site exclusively for your wedding—and even receive a discount—simply by holding your wedding on a Friday evening or Sunday afternoon.

Having your wedding in an off-season month might also guarantee you better service from your caterer. Brian and I, for example, held our wedding on June 5, one of the most popular wedding days of the year. Our caterer, who was also in charge of five other weddings that same day, seemed a bit harried. Although our reception was absolutely beautiful in every other way, half of our wine and champagne never made it to the reception and the linens we had ordered were nowhere to be seen. Ask ahead of time how busy your caterer anticipates being on the day of your wedding. If you are worried you will receive less than perfect service, you may want to choose another date (or another caterer).

WHERE

Choosing where to hold your wedding is a bit like deciding what type of wedding to throw. The possibilities are limitless. As you explore your options, keep in mind all of the decisions you've made so far. A fall wedding in Minnesota, for example, would be lovely; a winter wedding in Minnesota would not (when snowdrifts can reach as high as twenty-five feet). And while a sun-kissed wedding weekend in the Bahamas sounds idyllic, make sure that all of your closest (but maybe not richest) friends can afford the flight. Where you hold your wedding should be a reflection of what kind of wedding you are throwing, inspiring all of the feelings that are most important to you and your groom about your wedding day. This location, however, should also be appropriate for the time of year of your wedding and for all of your guests who may be traveling to support you on this special occasion.

Wedding Myth # 3: **The wedding has to be held in the bride's hometown**. *This was the old tradition. Nowadays, it can be held in the groom's hometown or anywhere in between.*

COUNTRY More and more brides and grooms these days are fleeing home to exchange their vows, and no, they're not eloping. They're inviting their friends and families to join them. I call these destination weddings, and again, space (as in outer) seems to be the limit thus far. Some brides are renting out Scottish castles, others are ferrying guests through Venetian canals to opulent waterfront parties, and yet another bride I know says she's in need of an itty-bitty island somewhere that doesn't even have a name yet.

If you've already found your itty-bitty island, be sure and research all travel rules and restrictions regarding overseas marriages (unlike other wedding rules, these are not optional). Check with the country's U.S. embassy or tourism bureau about residency requirements, proper documentation (including passports, visas, or birth certificates), medical tests, paperwork processing time, proof of divorce, witnesses, and the requirements for both religious and civil ceremonies. Many countries require that these documents be submitted both in English and the local language, so start the process as early as possible. Also make sure your airplane tickets are in your proper names. Some overzealous brides and grooms make their travel reservations in their newly married names, even before they are married. Airlines will not allow passengers to board if their ticket name does not match their identification name.

Many travel agents will have a list of your destination's wedding requirements and can help you reserve both your plane tickets and perhaps even a wedding officiant. Resorts and popular honeymoon hotels often have on-site coordinators who will also be able to help you plan your wedding, from ordering a cake and flowers to helping you decipher the country's specific marriage restrictions. And, welcome to the World Wide Web. Many on-line travel sites provide all the details for throwing a completely lavish—and completely legal—overseas wedding. Besides making your own travel arrangements, you should also be prepared to help your guests with hotel recommendations as well as providing them with information about the country they'll be traveling to. One creative bride designed her own web site, including information on hotels in the area, links to other web sites providing information and photographs of the country, and family trees and photographs of her and her groom's families. Guests were also able to submit their travel plans and view those of other guests.

Even if you are not planning an exotic island extravaganza, you will need to do a bit of research. Different states—even different counties—have their own marriage rules. Call the county marriage license department where you'll be holding the wedding and ask for guidelines regarding blood tests, birth certificates, and proof of divorce, as well as if there's a waiting period for using the marriage license (twenty-four hours in some counties) and how long the marriage license is valid. If you or your groom-to-be are from a foreign country, find out what other documents you may need to provide. You will also want to make sure a wedding in the United States is recognized in your or his home country. For instance, Anne discovered when she called the French consulate to change her passport name that just because she had been married in the United States didn't mean she was legally married in France (not a bad excuse to hold two weddings!).

CITY AND STATE If planning a wedding in a foreign country seems about as appropriate as planning one on Mars, you may want to stick to choosing a city and state. Maybe you would be most comfortable in your new hometown of Chicago, or maybe you look forward to returning home to your family's synagogue in Cincinnati. Again, keep in mind decisions you've already made. Laurie and Michael, for instance, both known for their quirky senses of humor, were excited about hosting a kitchy Vegas wedding complete with an Elvis officiant. However, when they realized their grandparents in Oklahoma wouldn't be able to make the trip, they quickly revised their plan. Instead, they rented out a fire hall in Tulsa, visited a local party store for decorations, and had the Elvis officiant flown in via helicopter. And nobody was more delighted than the grandparents, who had front-row seats.

What region of the country you hold your wedding in could also determine the cost of your wedding. Lisa and Shane, for instance, had their hearts set on a Manhattan wedding, but they were on a budget, and with the size of their guest list they knew it wasn't practical. Eventually, they decided to take a tour of sites on Long Island, just an hour's drive from Manhattan, where they found an elegant mansion that could accommodate all of their guests at almost half of what it would have cost to have their wedding in the city. They were able to invite all of their friends and family, and with the money they saved, splurged on spending their honeymoon night in a luxurious suite right on Central Park. "By being flexible about where to have our wedding," Lisa says, "we were able to include different parts of our dreams in different ways." Sometimes it's not so much where you have your wedding as who you celebrate it with that's important.

CEREMONY AND RECEPTION SITES Just as the time of day you hold your wedding indicates a certain level of formality, so does the wedding site you choose. Here are a few suggestions for a formal wedding, an informal wedding, and everything in between:

Ballrooms	Lofts	Cathedrals
Hotel banquet rooms	Museums	Mountaintop
Restaurants	City hall	Barn
Private rooms in clubs	Church	Field
and bars	Synagogue	Boat

Backyard	Historic sites or homes	Firehouse
Vineyard	College chapel	Roller coaster
Ice-skating rink	Under a tree	Private mansion
Cave	Hot-air balloon	Auditorium
Empire State Building	Riverbank	Park
Castle	Private home or	Ski lodge
Drive-thru window	apartment	Under a tent
Beach	Country club	A Vegas chapel of love
Golf course	Bed and breakfast	
Ranch	Zoo	

Choosing a unique location for your wedding means creating a unique and memorable event. But again, make sure the site you choose is appropriate, and most important, that it matches the size of your guest list. Fifty guests in a lavish ballroom will feel a little lost. Three hundred guests in a quaint bed and breakfast might feel as if they're in an overcrowded zoo. Talk with your reception-site manager about creating a space that is comfortable for your guests and will allow everyone to have a good time. You can't dance if you can't make it to the dance floor.

> *Wedding Myth* #4: **Outdoor weddings are more romantic than indoor weddings.** *Not if your wedding is in Texas in August, in Alaska in January, next to an airport, or downwind from a sewage plant. Be sure and check out your potential ceremony or reception site during the time of year and day of your wedding.*

Talking to your site manager also means asking some real questions. Welcome to the Best Friend's Reception Site Questionnaire. I've just provided the questions. Your reception-site manager will need to provide the answers. Remember, weddings consist of many, many details, and the more details your reception site takes care of—the more services they provide—the less headaches you'll be left with on the wedding day.

The Best Friend's Reception Site Questionnaire

- What is the basic fee for the reception site? Is the fee negotiable? What if I hold my wedding on a Sunday afternoon?

- What does the rental fee include? Are there any additional fees I should be aware of?

- How many hours does the fee cover? When does the time frame begin and end? Is there a minimum or maximum number of hours I must use the site? Is there a charge for extending this time?

- How many guests can the site comfortably fit—for a buffet? a sit-down dinner? Is there a maximum number of guests the site can hold?

- Can I hold my ceremony at the site? Will the staff change over the room from the ceremony to the reception?

- Will there be any weddings immediately before, after, or at the same time as mine? How do you keep the two functions separate?

- Are there any restrictions regarding flowers, decorations, candles, or photography?

- Are there any restrictions on what types of music or instruments can be played, or the duration of the music? Will I need to

register outdoor music with the local police? Is dancing allowed? Where? Are there adequate outlets and electricity for
lighting and a band? Will I need to rent a generator?

◆ Are podiums, microphones, and speakers available? Do you
have a sound system?

◆ Do you have an in-house caterer or a list of recommended caterers? Can I use an outside caterer instead of the in-house caterer if
I choose?

◆ Are there kitchen facilities for the caterer? (A caterer will charge
you for any appliances he may need to bring, including a stove
or a refrigerator.)

◆ Are tables, chairs, silverware, and barware available? Will I
need to rent these?

◆ Is parking available? Is it free? Can I arrange for valet parking?
Where should the caterer, band, and other vendors park?

◆ Can I set up a coat check for guests? Is there an extra room
where I can change? Are there any extra rooms the band can use
as dressing rooms? Is there a fee for these?

◆ Are there bathrooms? Where are they?

◆ Is there a dress code for guests?

◆ Is there a site manager or coordinator who will be at the site the
day of the wedding? Who should I see if I have any questions?
Will you need a schedule of when the other vendors are arriving? Can vendors contact you with questions regarding the site?

◆ What is the policy regarding furniture at the site? Can I arrange
to have it moved or can I move it myself? Who do I need to
contact?

- Do you provide a cleanup service or will I be in charge of this? How much time does cleanup take? Do you have a checklist of what needs to be cleaned? Do you provide cleaning supplies?

- Do you have security guards on site or will I need to hire my own?

- Do you have fire extinguishers? Where are they?

- Is the site air-conditioned? Does the site have heat?

- Do you have liability insurance in case a guest is injured?

- How much is the deposit? When is the balance due? Is there an extra security deposit? When is this refunded?

- Will you provide complimentary rooms?

- What are your cancellation and refund policies?

If you love your reception site, as well as the manager's answers, go ahead and reserve it (in fact, hurry up—popular wedding sites go quickly!). Review your list of questions and answers and work with the manager to draw up a contract. This should include:

- Your names (both bride's and groom's) and the exact time and date of the wedding.

- The total reception-site fee, including the deposit and when it was paid, the amount of the security deposit and when it will be refunded, and instructions for paying the balance.

- The name of the reception site and the exact rooms you will be using.

- What services the fee includes and any additional services you negotiated.

- All rules and restrictions for use of the property.

- The name of the site coordinator.

- The cancellation and refund policy.

Make sure your contract is as complete as possible. Your reception-site manager may change (especially if you are reserving your site a year or more in advance) and you want to make sure all agreements are in writing. You might also ask for references or talk to someone you know who has held their wedding at the same site, or check with the Better Business Bureau to see if any complaints were filed. You may even want to pay the deposit with a credit card. If your reception site goes out of business or refuses to honor your contract, your credit card company is legally required to investigate. They will be responsible for making sure the site covers the cost, not you. (Plus, think of all those extra frequent-flier miles!) All of this is not meant to scare you. But the reality is that while your wedding is your dream, your wedding is your reception site's (and every other vendor's) business. Simply think of each contract as a business deal and cover as many of those details as possible. Taking care of business beforehand means you will have nothing left to take care of—besides eating and drinking and laughing and dancing—on your wedding day.

And right after you've decided where to have your ceremony and reception, it's time to figure out a few more fun things—like how to get to your reception—and then drive off into the sunset. Both present wonderful opportunities to do something personal and creative. At Mike and Chrissie's Philadelphia wedding, for instance, the couple hired an antique trolley car to pick up the wedding party and drive around to some of the couple's favorite sites before heading to the reception. Awais, a Pakistani groom at a loss as to how to re-create the traditional Hindu *barat* (a lively groom's processional) in Austin, Texas, chartered a bus to take all the male guests (and their drums and cymbals and noisemakers) to the ceremony. Alan and Cindy married at the firehouse where Alan works and had engine Number 9 take everyone to dinner after the ceremony. One couple I've heard of left their reception in an eighteen-wheeler (not before a few good pulls on the horn, of course). Your "getaway car" need not be merely a car. Consider renting a bicycle built for two, a hot-air balloon, a horse-drawn carriage, water skis, snow skis . . . you get the idea.

So, do a little bit of research: Check your area for antique car clubs that might be willing to loan out a vintage car, peep around local farms that may have an old winter sleigh or carriage lying around. And if you wind up renting any vehicle and/or hiring a chauffeur for the day, make sure you draw up a contract that includes the following: exact vehicle; name of driver and telephone number; deposit fee; total cost; total number of hours of the rental; cancellation/refund policies; and date, time, and location of all events at which you'll need the vehicle and/or driver.

Also, don't forget that a getaway just isn't a getaway unless your guests have something to throw at you. Rice is a no-no these days, but consider birdseed, bubbles, butterflies, rose petals, or streamers. Anika's and Mike's parents actually arranged for a fireworks display across the river from their reception site as a grand finale to the weekend's festivities. "Mike's and my first date was on the Fourth of July in Washington, D.C. We both worked for members of Congress and the holiday has always been a special one for us. So, even though our wedding was in Minnesota, in October, our parents found a way to include a little bit of the Fourth. What a spectacular way to start a marriage!"

WHY

Because his mother wants us to, because my mother wants us to, because my friends would kill me if we didn't. Oh, just kidding (kind of). By now, you should have a clear idea of who you're throwing this wedding for, what kind of wedding you want it to be, and when and where the wedding will take place. Some brides, at this point (or just some brides' mothers), will feel tempted to pull out one of those unwieldy etiquette books and start hunting down all the rules on why your wedding plan may or may not be exactly proper. Maybe you really, really care about this. Or maybe it would be a lot more fun to come up with your own set of wedding rules.

Andrea and Michael came up with this unique idea while frantically attempting to reign in a wedding plan gone completely out of control. As to-do lists grew (along with the arguments), they both tried desperately to remember the "why" of it all. Creating a list of their own wedding rules helped. Via e-mail, Andrea typed up a list of what was absolutely important to her about their wedding day, and Michael responded with his own list. Including the very simple rule that they wind up husband and wife, their list soon became a guideline to refer to throughout the planning process. One quick glance would remind them of why there was no reason whatsoever to obsess over song lists and music, but why spending the extra time to write their ceremony and vows would mean a lot. Their list became a personal document of all their dreams and hopes for their wedding day—and it helped them make every one of them come true.

Your own list of wedding rules should be created early, when you both are laughing, excited, and still completely in love with the whole wedding process (i.e., when the idea of interviewing caterers and florists and photographers seems absolutely delightful). It should also be done when you're still in love with each other and way before you turn to the next chapter.

The Budget

IS THAT MONEY IN YOUR POCKET
OR ARE YOU JUST HAPPY TO SEE ME?

This chapter is all about various and sundry things like money, pockets, budgets, and happiness. Some of these things have everything to do with each other. Some of these things have absolutely nothing to do with each other. All of these things, however, have everything to do with weddings, and all of them must be talked about at some point with your groom, your family, and your groom's family. But before you dive right in, why don't we figure out exactly what it is you're going to be talking about?

MONEY

Money is one of those funny things that everybody seems to have their own definition of. I came up with my own theory regarding money a long time ago: "Give money generously, spend money gracefully, consider money gravely." When applied to weddings, I think the translation works out to be roughly: "Make sure you have enough money after the wedding to live." This should be your first hint that weddings can cost a lot of money and lead you to the very next thought: Where am I going to get all that money?

Wedding Myth #5: **Weddings have to be expensive.** *Some weddings are. Some weddings aren't. This is entirely up to you and your groom—not your caterer, florist, photographer, musicians, or mothers.*

POCKETS

Pockets are those funny little things often found in pants, skirts, dresses, shorts, and shirts where people keep that other funny thing we just talked about—money. In order to figure out with whom you will need to discuss the subject of money, you will first need to figure out from which set of pockets the money for your wedding will be coming.

If you and your groom-to-be will be footing the bill yourselves, flip through this chapter together, consider how deep or shallow your pockets are and, more important, what money means to both of you and why. Paying for a wedding may be the first thing you and your groom-to-be have ever actually paid for (or at least budgeted for) together. And while discussing why you *must* have that $4,000 sequined wedding dress and he *must* have that $4,000 country-and-western band may seem like a frustrating (and futile) exercise, remind yourselves that this will be the first of many, many conversations regarding money. You are not only planning a wedding, you are planning a marriage—a marriage of hearts, minds, bodies, and, well, pocketbooks. So while money doesn't necessarily buy happiness, agreeing on money can. Review your wedding plan carefully (who is this day for? what do you want it to feel like? why are you doing this exactly?) and take stock of those pockets of yours before deciding on how much you both feel comfortable spending on your wedding.

Adding your parents' pockets to your pockets means, of course, that you'll have a bit more money to spend on your wedding. It also means being a bit more careful about how you spend it. Hint: Bankrupting your future in-laws may not be the best way to introduce yourself to the family. So what is the best way? With tact, honesty, and respect. You may never have to budget for an event with your family or his ever again, but you will certainly see them again, and how you communicate and get along with your families now can very well affect your future relationships.

Accepting your families' financial help means accepting and respecting their opinions. Compromise is possible. However, don't feel pressured to compromise away your wedding day. Lily and David, for example, ran into a bit of trouble when David's dad handed over his half of the guest list with well over 100 names. He didn't understand Lily and David's protests: If he could afford to pay for a large wedding, why shouldn't they have one? The answer—because Lily and David didn't want one. In coming up with their wedding plan, they had envisioned a small, intimate gathering of their closest family and friends. Their dream was to spend quality time with the people they cared for the most, rather than spending time shaking the hands of people they'd never met. David's father eventually understood their dream and later admitted he was much happier getting busy on the dance floor with his family than he would have been worrying about introducing his family to his business friends.

Many brides and grooms split up their wedding bill by having the bride's family pay for certain events and items while the groom's family pays for others. Traditionally, the groom's family took care of such costs as the bride's and bridesmaids' bouquets, the rehearsal dinner, and honeymoon. The bride's family paid for the ceremony, reception, and boutonnieres for the groomsmen. However, when one family's pockets aren't quite as deep as the other's, this can become a problem. Trina's mother, for example, was embarrassed by the way the groom's family kept volunteering to pay for things—first the engagement party, then the rehearsal dinner. And although Trina and Lou had requested that guests make contributions to charity in lieu of gifts, every time she showed up at the couple's new apartment there was yet another gift from the groom's mother. She and her husband certainly weren't as well off as the groom's parents, but she was ultimately confused and hurt that nobody asked her or her husband for help. The wedding was a large celebration of both families' heritages, but Trina's mother couldn't help but feel the wedding belonged to Lou's family. In retrospect, Trina says she and Lou should have stood by their original plan: accepting everyone's ideas but paying for everything themselves.

Maria and Stephan are a couple who took particular care not to let their wedding plan spin out of control. They sat down with both of their families at the very beginning and talked candidly about their dream for their wedding and how much everyone could afford to spend. Stephan's family agreed to pay a third. Maria's family paid a third. And Maria and Stephan themselves paid a third. The couple immediately put their parents' money and the money they had saved into a separate banking account. That way, Maria says, they could pay for everything as they went along. She didn't have to make calls back and forth negotiating with her mother or wait for Stephan to call and confirm a cost with his father. She notes, "A wedding may be romantic—but paying for one never is. I wanted to make things as simple as possible, and I think everyone appreciated how open and businesslike Stephan and I were. I do know everyone was proud. My mother came up to me during the reception and said, 'Wow, we helped pay for all of this?'"

> *Wedding Myth* # 6: *You will receive enough monetary gifts to pay for your wedding.* This is completely false (even if you return your fine china). You may receive enough to pay for your honeymoon, but don't count on it.

Working with your family and his family to pay for a wedding can be complicated, especially given the size of many families today. It is not unusual for a couple to be dealing with fathers, mothers, stepmothers, stepfathers—perhaps even two of each. And every one of those people might have a different vision or dream or idea for your wedding day. Happily, weddings are custom-made events. You can include parts of your mother's dream, one or two of his stepmother's ideas, even a little of his stepfather's vision. After all, everyone's money is helping to put this wedding together. And what better way to thank everyone for his or her help than by including everyone in this very special day?

Of course, before everyone begins smiling like idiots and happily emptying their pockets, someone (perhaps even you) is going to ask the inevitable: How much is this whole thing going to cost me? That brings us to another interesting word . . .

BUDGET

A budget, on the surface of things, is basically a sheet of paper made up of two columns. In one column is a list of each item you will need to pay for at this little (or large) wedding of yours. In the other column are blanks for the amounts of money you will need to pay for each of these items. At the very end of this column is a blank for the total amount of money you will be spending for all of the items combined. This sheet of paper may actually seem rather simple until you try to fill in the blanks. You then immediately realize there is more to this whole budget thing than meets the eye: It's called math. *Math? But I don't do math*. Me neither, so I called my sister, Shelley, who happens to do math rather well, for some help. This is how she explained it to me:

A basic wedding budget is made up of six main categories, each accounting for a certain percentage of the total sum spent. In general, she estimates that food and beverage should amount to 50 percent of your wedding cost; flowers, 8 percent; music, 12 percent; photography, 10 percent; attire, 10 percent; and miscellaneous, 10 percent. The miscellaneous category is comprised of various items such as marriage license and officiant fees, blood tests, invitations, stamps, thank-you notes, programs, place cards, favors, tips, attendant gifts, limousine fees, reception- and ceremony-site fees, wedding rings, and your cake, if it isn't included in your caterer's food and beverage cost. This category is where most budgets tend to run over ("Oops, you mean we have to pay for all those napkins and matchbooks with our names on them?"), so you may want to allot a little more, say 15 percent, of your total budget just to be on the safe side. You and your groom may also choose to spend a little more or a little less in certain categories you care more—or less—about.

Shelley also cautions that if your wedding is a long-distance affair, you'll also need to consider the cost of plane tickets (plan on an average of two trips) and all of those long-distance phone calls you're about to start making. Couples should expect to call their vendors at least every other week once the wedding draws near just to see how things are coming along, their mothers every hour or so just to let them know how things are coming along, and their best friends every five minutes or so just to see what's going on in the real world. In general, the price of life will go up during the planning of your wedding. These costs may be difficult to estimate, but you will definitely want to keep them in mind.

What is easy to estimate, Shelley promised, is your main wedding budget, since each category is in some way or another related to the others and affects their cost. For instance, most caterers will give you a price based on a cost per person. Hence, if you are quoted a fee of $100 per person, your 300-person guest list will cost you $30,000. The more people you add to your guest list, the more you pay for food—and the more you pay for almost every aspect of the wedding. More guests mean more invitations, more stamps, more programs, more tables, more linens, more flower arrangements—more of just about everything.

The first step in coming up with a budget, then, is to determine the size of your guest list. This exercise is fundamentally about math, too, so I had Shelley take me through it step-by-step. First, she says, have your family, your groom's family, and you and your groom write down the name of every single person you and they can possibly think of who might want to come to the wedding. Count each name, multiplying single guests by two if you think they'd like to bring a guest (hint: they will). Add up everybody's lists. Apologize for giving your dad a heart attack and immediately subtract all the people who may really want to come to the wedding but aren't going to be invited anyway. This sometimes takes a few days (or weeks) of arguing, so give yourself some time on this one. After all the fiddling and fussing, however, you should have an appropriately sized guest list that pretty much pleases everybody.

Of course, you might already have in mind the perfect-sized guest list. In this case, divide this number by two (he and his family invite half the total number; you and your family invite half the total number) or three (you and your groom invite a third; his family invites a third; your family invites a third) or four—you get the idea. Have each family count, add, multiply, subtract, and argue on their own until they've each come up with the specific number they were assigned. This sometimes leaves you out of the fiddling and fussing process altogether, but not always. Here's the key: Blame it on math, i.e., "I'm really sorry, Mrs. Smith, but I've gone over and over the figures, and with the optimum number of guests set at one hundred fifty, and your fraction of the integer equal to a number not more than but equal to fifty, mathematically, it just doesn't compute that you can invite a sum of seventy-three guests." She will either understand this completely, or she will be so confused she won't know what to say. A pretty nice concept, huh?

Yep, Shelley says, math is much nicer than anyone gives it credit for—much easier, too. Because once you've figured out your guest list, filling in the blanks of your budget becomes a breeze. Say, for instance, you've arrived at a guest list of 200. Call up the caterer you're considering and get an approximate cost per person. Multiply this number by 200 (this is approximately how much you'll spend on food and beverage).

Then, since your food costs are approximately 50 percent of your total budget, multiply this number by two. This will give you a general idea of how much you are going to need to spend on your wedding (at this point, feel free to add in costs for the honeymoon and any additional events you'll be throwing, such as a rehearsal dinner). If this number causes your dad to have yet another heart attack, you have two options: Cut down your guest list, or cut down your catering costs.

If you simply must have all 200 members of your family at your wedding (you have a *really* big family), consider hosting an afternoon buffet lunch rather than an evening sit-down dinner. Or check on serving wine, beer, and champagne only rather than an open bar. Caterers can be wizards at shaving off food and beverage costs that most guests won't even notice. However, if it's more important to you and your groom to serve the finest foods in the most luxurious of settings, work with your parents to trim the guest list. You might also decide to cut down on costs within each category, but remember that food and beverage really do have the largest effect on your wedding's cost. No matter how many guests are invited, a fancy dinner generally means more sophisticated (read: more expensive) invitations, music, and décor than if you were to host a casual mid-morning brunch for just as many people. While negotiating special deals may save you money in other areas, cutting your food cost is the number one way to cut down on your budget. So, mull it over (leave enough time for this, too), re-add, re-multiply, and re-subtract as needed, until everyone whose pockets you'll be picking is satisfied.

After that, the rest of the blanks practically fill in themselves. Shelley shows us how with these easy formulas:

TOTAL # OF GUESTS X PRICE PER PERSON X 2 = TOTAL COST
TOTAL COST X .50 = FOOD
TOTAL COST X .08 = FLOWERS
TOTAL COST X .12 = MUSIC
TOTAL COST X .10 = PHOTOGRAPHY

TOTAL COST X .10 = ATTIRE

TOTAL COST X .10 = MISCELLANEOUS

Suddenly, filling in all of those blanks on that sheet of paper called your budget doesn't seem so difficult. Afterward, you might even begin to ponder such questions as "How many flowers will $1,000 buy?," "Are engraved invitations really as expensive as everyone says?," "How big a band can I afford for $2,500 and where do I find one?" These are all very good questions and we'll get to each of them in the chapters that follow. But first, we have one last funny little thing to talk about.

> *Wedding Myth* # 7: **Once you have created a budget, you will know how to stay on a budget.** *No one ever stays on a budget. Girls: Don't buy a whole new wardrobe for your honeymoon. Boys: Rent—don't buy—the vintage car for your reception getaway.*

HAPPINESS

Way, way back, oh, fifty pages or so, you were happy. Life was simple. Weddings were silly. Now, one proposal, two or three phone calls to friends and family, and four or five brainstorming sessions later, regarding music and menus and marriage licenses, and life isn't so simple— even that wedding that was once so ridiculous now seems very, very important. It may also suddenly seem very, very important to spend a lot of money on your wedding. In fact, there is a theory running rampant that the more money you spend, the better the wedding and the happier you will be. This is absolutely not true, and to prove it I'd like to talk about two wonderful weddings—and one very wonderful bride.

At Gina's first wedding, friends and family flew in from all over the world for an elaborate ceremony in one of the most beautiful temples in town. The couple exchanged vows under a stunning *chuppa* draped with intricately embroidered cloth brought over by Gina's family in Israel, and the rabbi, a close friend of her parents, gave moving readings in both English and Hebrew. Afterward, guests were treated to a reception even more elaborate than the ceremony. No expense was spared: The foods and wines were the best money could buy. The cake came from the best baker in town. Gina's dress came from the best designer. The flowers came from the best florist. And the band, flown in from across the country, played well into the night. The photographer (also the best in town) took stunning photographs of all of the guests smiling, laughing, and having an absolutely fabulous (i.e., the best) time.

But looking back on the day, Gina says she felt like an actress: "The wedding really was wonderful, and I know my parents still think this was the kind of wedding I wanted. But they chose absolutely everything—the food, the cake, even my dress. I remember looking around and thinking that nothing in that room had anything to do with me. I was so young, though, I'm not sure I even knew who that 'me' was."

Gina's marriage (like her wedding) didn't work out all that well, which is why she just recently had a second wedding. This wedding was also wonderful, but in a completely different way. "I was ten years older and I knew so much more about myself and my tastes. Scott and I didn't spend a lot of money, but we picked out exactly what we wanted. I was completely relaxed and I didn't worry about all of the little details. I simply kept thinking about the big picture—about what I had come to know about marriage and love—and the day turned out perfectly. It was spiritual, and even more important, real."

So which wedding was better? I'll leave you to figure that out on your own, but here's a hint: The answer has nothing to do with how much either wedding cost but with how much love was spent planning and celebrating the wedding.

After the Plan

YOUR GROOM AND WHAT TO DO WITH HIM

Your groom-to-be loves you. In fact, he loves you so much, he asked you to marry him. Or maybe you asked him to marry you, and he loves you so much, he said yes. In any case, your groom-to-be loves you, but this may or may not mean he will love your wedding, or the planning of your wedding. In fact, after awhile, even the word "wedding" may cause him to exhibit any number of bizarre types of behavior, including stuttering and sweating when confronted with a seemingly easy question such as, "Did you have a chance to call the caterer today?"; painful moaning sounds when re-asked the seemingly easy question, "Did you have a chance to call the caterer today?"; frantic shouting and screaming that somehow translates into, "OKAY, OKAY, I'LL CALL THE CATERER TODAY!"; or a complete lack of stuttering, sweating, moaning, or shouting, which is usually evidence that he has disappeared altogether.

But we just came up with our wedding plan, you say, *we even made up our own completely romantic wedding rules.* I know, it's confusing, but the sad fact is that that was then and this is now. For some odd reason it's hard for grooms-to-be to maintain their enthusiasm for the six to twelve months it takes to plan a wedding. Now, this is not to say that there aren't some helpful, considerate, even reliable grooms out there. I have actually met two of them. Here are their stories:

WHAT GOOD GROOMS LOOK LIKE

Motivated

"Fumiko and I had just gotten engaged when my mother called to say my father was extremely ill. Suddenly, Fumiko was on the phone making travel arrangements for her family in Japan, and I was put in charge of planning our wedding. With just two weeks to prepare, I reserved a church, an organist, and a reception hall and placed about thirty phone calls before finding a DJ, photographer, and caterer who were available at such short notice. It was a little hectic getting everything done in two weeks, and there was the added stress that Fumiko's family didn't speak English and mine didn't speak Japanese. But everything came together perfectly, and music, as it turns out, is a universal language. I think I even saw my father tapping his foot."—JOSEPH

Sensitive

"The most important thing to me about our wedding was that Chrissie be able to relax and enjoy the weekend, so I volunteered to take care of all the last-minute details. I coordinated the delivery and set up times among vendors and made sure I was on hand in case anything went wrong. I also took charge of the decorations and lighting for the wedding. I own a special-effects lighting company, so I was able to hire vendors that I knew would make our wedding vision come true. Chrissie still says walking into the church and banquet hall was like walking into a wonderful surprise. What was wonderful for me was watching her walk in."—MICHAEL

If your fiancé happens to resemble these grooms, consider yourself lucky and feel free to skip to the next chapter. Unfortunately, most grooms-to-be seem to be more likely to take off than to take charge.

How do I know this? I asked them. Speak up, I said. Be heard. This is what they said.

Wedding Myth # 8: **Your groom's opinion doesn't count.** Um, this is his wedding, too. Plus, he might even have a good idea or two. I said might.

WHAT MOST GROOMS LOOK LIKE

Confused

"I don't think I was thinking at all (wait, that sounds weird, doesn't it?). I mean, I had just spent so much time and energy thinking about the engagement and planning the proposal and sitting up at night thinking about asking this amazing woman to be my wife (that's huge, you know; it was intense), that after she said yes, my brain just sort of shut off. I didn't understand any of the wedding plans our families were making, which I think everybody noticed because they put me in charge of the honeymoon and told me not to worry about anything else."—BILL

Curious

"I knew the wedding was important to her and her mother and my mother because they talked about it a lot. Every time I walked into the room she was on the phone talking about 'the caterer this,' 'the florist that,' and the seating chart, oh, the seating chart. The only thing I had any real interest in was seeing her come down the aisle (it was pretty amazing, you know). And I was curious about the dress, too, but the groom's not supposed to know anything about that." —MARTIN

Cautious

"I was given this advice before my wedding and now I'll give it to all grooms. Don't think at all. It only upsets everybody. Show bad taste at the beginning of the whole planning process and you'll never be asked your opinion again. It definitely worked for me." —JOHN

Diplomatic

"The wedding is two people's day: the bride's and her mother's. Do everything possible to make both of them happy and you will come through the whole event alive and pretty much happy. If she has a younger brother, get on his good side, because he has probably spent most of his life trying to make both of them happy and can give you advice. If she has an older brother, steer clear. Same thing with the father. They could care less if you two wind up married." —DANA

Opinionated

"There is this weird myth that I keep hearing that grooms don't care about the wedding plans. That's not at all true. We just don't care about the silly things. I made sure I was in charge of the important things: the band and the bar. No one's going to notice if a few of your tables don't have flower arrangements (none of the guys anyway), but everyone will notice if you have a lousy band or a cash bar after your cocktail hour. It just looks cheap. It's my philosophy that if you keep your guests drinking and dancing, everyone will have a good time." —TIM

Desperate

"I just wanted to get married." —CLINT

Okay, so maybe I didn't exactly catch these grooms-to-be at their most eloquent. Your fiancé may have some rather strange things to say about your own wedding, but, in some weird way or another, if you read between the lines, your groom-to-be really is thinking about you. My advice? Let him slide. Let him be stupid (just this once), because sooner or later you're going to need the same leeway. Meanwhile, here are some tips for dealing with your groom-to-be.

Wedding Myth # 9: **Your groom's family's opinion doesn't count.** *Your groom's family's opinion always counts. Especially if you want to wind up married.*

WHAT TO DO WITH YOUR GROOM

DON'T TALK TO EVERYBODY *BUT* THE GROOM-TO-BE ABOUT THE WEDDING. If you spend all your time giggling with your bridesmaids and sister and his mother and his sister, even his aunt, about the wedding plans, your fiancé may feel he's not really a part of the whole event—and will eventually start acting that way. If you've never asked him whether he'd like to have sparklers at each guest's place setting for your Fourth of July wedding, it's a bit unfair to expect him to act overly excited about driving two hours to the next state (fireworks are illegal in yours) to pick up 200 white sparklers (not blue) and 200 yards of blue ribbon (not white) to tie them up with. So ask your groom-to-be what he thinks—and more important, listen.

DON'T ONLY TALK ABOUT THE WEDDING. Don't forget you have a life. As a bride, most people will assume your life is about the wedding. They will corner you in bathrooms with questions like "So, have you registered yet?," "Ooooh, I bet your dress is beautiful, what does it look like?," or "All done with those invitations? I keep checking my mailbox!" For some reason, no one asks the groom these same questions, so although your life may begin to feel like it's about the wedding, remind yourself and your groom that it's not. Spend a whole day without talking about flower arrangements or menus. Instead, hold hands and talk about your future together. Or, simply kiss and stop talking altogether.

BE SPECIFIC. Your groom-to-be (or any other member of your family for that matter) is not a mind reader. Just because you are going to need him on Wednesday to go by the caterer (for the third time that week) to show him (again) the linens you both picked out four months ago doesn't mean he knows this. He might even make plans to have a beer with the boys if you don't hurry up and tell him. For any errand you need your groom to do, you will need to give him exact instructions, including addresses, phone numbers, directions, maps (heck, you might as well give him the cell phone and talk him through it), and anything else you can think of that he may need to get the job done. Oh, and don't forget to tell him why he's doing all this: It will make you very, very happy.

KEEP A SENSE OF HUMOR. Believe it or not, some men assume their brides-to-be actually enjoy running around to caterers and videographers and tasting cakes and frosting and waiting for callbacks from the florist and deciding whether to have black-and-white or color pictures taken, or both and how many of each. They honestly believe we take all of this seriously. Assure your groom-to-be you don't. In fact, promise each other that you'll laugh at least once a day at the whole silly process. Weddings are a lot more enjoyable if the planning seems more like fun and games than a business venture. Follow a meeting with your caterer with dinner at your favorite Mexican restaurant, or take a long lunch hour during the middle of the week to register (when the store is less crowded anyway) and pretend you're playing hooky. A wedding, at times, can seem like a disease. Laughter is always the best med-icine.

TELL HIM YOU LOVE HIM. And show him you love him.

Wedding Myth # 10: **Men don't cry.** *Yes, they do. And it's really sweet (just don't tell them that).*

Planning a wedding with your groom-to-be may seem like a recipe for disaster. The date you've picked out to meet with the caterer doesn't work for him. The date he's picked out to interview the DJ doesn't work for you. And speaking of dates, you can't remember the last time you and your groom-to-be went on one. What's going on? It's called a wedding and if the process seems crazy, it's because it is. So why are you doing it? Because not very long ago (six chapters ago to be exact), this same stuttering, moaning, shouting boy got down on one knee and stuttered out the sweetest, most beautiful proposal in the world. You're doing it because he loves you. Because you love him. And because it's good practice for a little thing called marriage.

The Attendants

WHO'S IN, WHO'S OUT

Good news: Friends are cool. They say cool things, do cool things, and can always, always be counted on for tons of cool advice. That's why I named this book *The Best Friend's Guide to Planning a Wedding* in the first place. Because without all of the cool things my friends said ("You're engaged? Yippee! Let's celebrate!") and did (throw me a shower with an unbelievably scrumptious banana cake), without all of their cool advice ("Yes, I'm pretty sure it's okay to have cheese grits even though it's an evening wedding"), I don't think I could ever have wound up married. Okay, maybe I would have wound up married, but I certainly wouldn't have had half as much fun doing it without them. Ultimately, this is what choosing attendants is all about: picking people you love to help you celebrate your wedding, help you face the problems planning a wedding involves, and most important, help you have fun along the way.

Bad news: Friends can be uncool. They can say uncool things, do uncool things, and can sometimes give some very uncool (and pretty weird) advice. One of Lori's childhood friends, for instance, told her, "I don't think you should be marrying Ben. He doesn't really love you." Debrah's sister didn't even show up the day of her wedding. And when Martine asked her friend if the date of the wedding worked for her, she replied, "Well, my daughter might be at camp that weekend and you know I'd really like her to be at the wedding. Maybe you could have the wedding in the town that's nearby so I could pick her up more easily." Huh?

Wedding Myth # 11: **Just because you were in a friend's wedding means she has to be in yours.** *If this were true, I know several brides who would have to have upward of thirty bridesmaids. Choose only your closest friends and family members. Everyone else will be happy to be guests.*

Weddings can be unbelievably special and beautiful occasions. But they can also be a bit overwhelming, even weird, for friends who may feel as if they're losing a best friend, or that while you've suddenly been blessed with love and happiness, they've been cursed with the prospect of buying yet another bridesmaid dress. Weddings involve lots of different kinds of people feeling lots of different kinds of emotions. They also involve two things that always seem to be in short supply: time and money, both of which you are about to ask your attendants to spend generously on you. So, expect a little whining, even a few revolts ("No, I will not wear pink taffeta"), but also expect all of the help, advice, love, and attention you could ever wish for. Your attendants are your friends, and that's what friends are for.

WHO THEY ARE AND WHAT THEY DO FOR YOU

The very first attendants you and your groom are likely to choose are your bridesmaids and groomsmen, but before you start picking friends and family willy-nilly, consider who you think will best play the following roles.

BEST MAN The best man is the official "I got it" man. The ring? He's got it. The marriage license? He's got it. The bow tie? He's got it. The socks? Yep, he's got those, too. Obviously, the best man needs to be someone really, really intelligent and someone really, really close to the groom (i.e., brother, best friend, stepfather). Because after the groom pulls off something as monumental as a marriage proposal, he'll immediately start acting like an idiot, which means the best man will immediately have to start thinking for him, as well as start apologizing to the bride for the groom's behavior. Of course, the best man also has to assure the groom that his behavior is perfectly acceptable, that all grooms get nervous a couple of months before the wedding, that all grooms stay out drinking till all hours a few weeks before the wedding, that all grooms disappear to the golf course for a quick thirty-six holes the day before the wedding, and a variety of other things that may or may not be true but that the groom will want to hear anyway. The ability to be flexible with the truth often comes in handy here.

The best man's other official duties may include:

- helping groom pick out his wedding attire (makes sure it's not too embarrassing)

- helping groom pick out groomsmen's attire (makes sure it's not too expensive)

- hosting bachelor party (remembers to ask groom what he really wants and makes sure all male relatives of the bride and groom are invited)

- helping coordinate other groomsmen's transportation and lodging at the wedding

- attending rehearsal and rehearsal dinner (makes sure other groomsmen attend)

- standing next to groom during ceremony

- holding bride's wedding band during ceremony

- escorting best lady down aisle after ceremony

- signing marriage certificate

- keeping checks for reception vendors and extra cash for tipping and bribing

- standing in receiving line and sitting at head table

- giving toast (uses no notes, makes three points, includes mentions of both bride and groom, and saves embarrassing the groom for the bachelor party)

- dancing with best lady during formal first dance

- dancing with all mothers throughout the evening (keeps all single women happy by dancing with them, too)

- making sure waiters and bartenders know who bride, groom, and their families are (in other words, makes sure everyone—especially groom—has a drink at all times)

- dealing with reception foul-ups (if band is too loud, tells them to turn it down; if caterer runs out of red wine, runs out to buy more)

- managing friction (makes sure families, friends, bridesmaids, and groomsmen do not hurt each other or sleep together)

- returning groom's and/or other groomsmen's rental attire (tracks down all bow ties, shoes, vests, suspenders, handkerchiefs, etc.)

- being an all around, super-duper, good ole funny guy

GROOMSMEN The rest of the groom's fan club, the groomsmen are basically there to do anything the groom or the best man (or anyone else, for that matter) tells them. They help plan the bachelor party and any other wedding events (golf tournament, softball game, coed shower); they arrange to pay for and pick up their wedding-day attire; they attend the rehearsal and rehearsal dinner; they serve as ushers; they escort the bridesmaids during either the processional or recessional (or both); and they stand next to the groom during the wedding ceremony, offering him their unfailing support.

The groomsmen are also responsible for performing several smaller duties, which may include: bringing tissues for the mothers during the rehearsal and rehearsal dinner (those toasts can get pretty sappy), making people (and especially the groom) laugh, dancing with the bridesmaids if there is a formal first dance (and then continuing to dance with anyone and everyone all night long), reserving a couple of bottles of champagne for the wedding party (hiding them if necessary), and carrying out any wedding pranks. Kidnapping the bride and taking her on an impromptu tour of the city's basketball courts in full wedding attire, decorating the getaway car, writing "help me" on the bottom of the groom's shoes for guests to read while he kneels, and/or substituting the breakable glass with a shatterproof one are all tried-and-true options.

But most important, it is the groomsmen's job to act as if nothing out of the ordinary whatsoever is happening. In other words, just because their friend is (gasp) getting married doesn't mean they won't all remain best friends (whew).

> *Wedding Myth* # 12: **You do not have to ask your groom who you can have in your wedding party.** *Talk to your groom about who your attendants will be way before you actually invite anybody to be in your wedding. Otherwise, your groom could wind up with ten attendants and you could wind up with three.*

BEST LADY The best lady (much easier and a lot more fun to say than maid or matron of honor) is the official "I'll take care of it" person. Trying to figure out how to spread the word regarding where you're registered? She'll take care of it. Need to pick up your place cards from the calligrapher but just can't seem to fit it into your schedule? She'll take care of it. It's two hours before the ceremony and you realize you forgot to pick up a very important prescription for the honeymoon? She'll take care of it. But the number one thing the best lady takes care of is the bride, acting as head cheerleader ("yes, you can do this"), therapist ("yes, it's perfectly normal to feel like you can't"), and mind reader ("no, you can't run off to Mexico to think about it"). The best lady, then, should know the bride very, very well. A sister, best friend, or mother are all good choices, someone who is likely to have seen the bride exhibit outlandish behavior in the past and won't be too shocked when she starts running around like a wacko wedding woman (it happens).

The best lady's other duties may include:

- helping bride pick out wedding dress (makes sure she doesn't faint from the excitement)

- helping bride pick out bridesmaids' dresses, shoes, and jewelry (makes sure bridesmaids don't faint from the expense)

- hosting bridal shower and/or bachelorette party (remembers to ask bride what she really wants and makes sure all female relatives of the bride and groom are invited)

- helping coordinate transportation and lodging for other bridesmaids (offers to make hotel reservations for everyone to guarantee their rooms will be together, or, if wedding is in her hometown, offers to have bridesmaids stay with family and friends)

- attending bridesmaids' luncheon (checks bride's state of mind)

- attending rehearsal and rehearsal dinner (double-checks bride's state of mind)

- spending the night with bride before wedding (restores her state of mind)

- helping bride get ready for ceremony (tells her she is so beautiful there is absolutely no way her groom won't cry)

- walking down aisle before bride

- straightening bride's veil and fluffing train after her processional

- holding groom's wedding band during ceremony

- holding bride's bouquet while bride and groom exchange vows and rings

- processing back down aisle with best man

- signing marriage certificate

- helping bride prepare for reception (removes or cuts off bride's veil, ties bustle, and gives her the biggest, tightest hug in the whole world—without wrinkling either of their dresses)

- standing in receiving line and sitting at head table

- giving toast (uses no notes, makes three points, includes mention of both bride and groom, and saves tears for very end of toast)

- dancing with best man during formal first dance

- dancing with all grandfathers, flower girls, ring bearers

- making sure bride eats (sneaks her crackers throughout the reception and makes sure caterer packs a meal—and a piece of cake—to go)

- dealing with reception foul-ups (bride's heel just broke? convinces her to take them off and let the real fun begin)

- managing friction (makes sure families, friends, bridesmaids, and groomsmen do not hurt each other or sleep together)

- helping bride change into getaway clothes (carries luggage to getaway car)

- helping parents collect gifts at end of reception (helps collect parents at end of reception)

- being an unfailingly lovely, gracious, cheerful, happy, smiling guardian angel

BRIDESMAIDS If the best lady is the bride's head cheerleader, think of the bridesmaids as the rest of the squad. They help the best lady plan the bridal shower and bachelorette party; they purchase their dresses, shoes, and any jewelry the bride has requested; they attend the bridesmaids' luncheon, rehearsal, and rehearsal dinner; they help the bride get ready, process down the aisle before her, and support her at the altar or *chuppa*. They may or may not stand in a receiving line, sit at a head table at the reception, or dance with the groomsmen during a formal first dance. But they absolutely do line up behind the best lady for the conga line and do their best to keep the dance floor crowded all night long.

Bridesmaids also serve some very important, individual roles. Consider which of the following bridesmaids you may need at your own wedding:

- PRACTICAL BRIDESMAID: Comes up with solutions to all wedding (and sometimes nonwedding) emergencies. Often brings an emergency kit along for the bride (including such important items as extra hose, emery board, dental floss, aspirin, and mints) and takes such emergency measures as propping overheated bride over air-conditioning vent.

- ◆ FUN BRIDESMAID: Keeps bride laughing when practical solutions don't work. Often brings along radio and music for bride and bridesmaids to get ready to and some kind of tasty food and beverages for the wedding party to snack on during preparations.

- ◆ CALM BRIDESMAID: Makes sure bride doesn't laugh so hard she becomes hysterical. Often acts as the designated hand holder and volunteers to take care of any last-minute preparations: putting together wedding programs, running back to the bride's house for the forgotten reception favors, helping unroll aisle runner.

- ◆ RESPONSIBLE BRIDESMAID: Keeps track of all bride's and bridesmaids' belongings, staying behind to clean up dressing room if necessary. Often helps florist pass out bridesmaids' bouquets and mothers' and grandmothers' corsages. Always put in charge of tracking RSVPs for bridal shower and/or bachelorette party.

There are no rules as to how many bridesmaids you will need or want. Some brides just wouldn't be able to stand up at the altar without every single one of their friends standing beside them. Some brides realize that every single one of their friends would probably kill one another before any one of them made it up to the altar. Know your friends, know yourself, and be kind, considerate, and honest with all of them.

Wedding Myth # 13: ***Your attendants are your slaves.*** *While friends and family will be happy to help you with your wedding plans, they should never take the place of a wedding coordinator or planner. Tip: Spend the extra money; keep your friends.*

Of course, there are all sorts of other roles your friends and family can play in your wedding. So, if you have a large family, or just feel the need to surround yourself with as many friends as possible on the big day, consider having the following attendants: honorary bridesmaids and groomsmen, junior bridesmaids and groomsmen, a ring bearer, a flower girl, a guest book attendant, a program attendant, ushers, *chuppa* holders, a cross bearer, a candle lighter, readers, and soloists. The important thing to keep in mind about all of these attendants is that they're your friends. Hint: You don't want to lose them, which is why you have a few things you need to do for them, too.

WHAT YOU DO FOR THEM

Although it may seem hard to believe, not everyone has been a bridesmaid or groomsman or ring bearer before. So while your friends and family may be thrilled and honored to be included in your wedding, they may not know what's expected of them. It's your job to tell them. As you ask your friends to be a part of your wedding (and, hints one bride, ask them at the same time, because they *will* talk to each other), make sure to give them the big picture as soon as possible: when you'll want them to arrive, all scheduled activities for the week or weekend, appropriate attire for each event. And as your wedding plan takes shape, be sure to update them. This is where e-mail comes in handy, especially if your friends live all over the country—or even the world. Send out regular "wedding newsletters" to your wedding party, updating them on the big day. Friends will be excited to be included in the planning process and happy to respond to your questions and concerns with wedding advice of their own.

Friends are also always very excited to know you're taking care of them on the financial front. Travel, accommodations, meals, wedding attire, wedding gifts—all of these things add up, and it's important to be sensitive and considerate of your attendants' pockets. You should respect any friend's decision not to be included as an attendant—the choice was probably a painful one. But you should also think of ways to help out. If at all possible, arrange for places for your bridesmaids and groomsmen to stay. If you're getting married in your hometown, ask Mom how full the house will be with relatives—and enlist the hospitality of neighbors and friends. If friends and family will need to stay at a hotel, reserve a block of rooms at one or two hotels in the area. By assuring the hotel a certain number of guests, they will often offer a discount to guests who call by a certain date. Be sure to include this information in all of your out-of-town guests' wedding invitations or in a separate mailing. And let your wedding party know as soon as possible—they wouldn't want to miss that deadline. Also be sure to ask your friends and family members with children if they'd like you to reserve them a suite, a room with a refrigerator or even a kitchen, and/or a room next to the pool.

Friends and family with smaller children may need even more attention. Ask if they'd like you to reserve a baby-sitter for the ceremony, the reception, or both, and make sure to get the total number of children to be looked after before calling one or more baby-sitters. Many parents, however, may prefer that their children attend both the ceremony and the reception, and if you know your reception is likely to be busy with young folks, enlist a baby-sitter to watch over them throughout the evening. Set up a kids' table, equipped with crayons, coloring books (perhaps even a paper tablecloth), fun, kid-friendly favors, and, of course, tons of tasty treats.

The weekend of your wedding, activities are likely to be rather segregated. The guys gather for a round of golf, a game of bowling, or a never-ending dart tournament at a local watering hole. And the girls, well, the girls have a party. This is called the bridesmaids' luncheon and it's your opportunity to thank everyone for being in your wedding. A friend or relative might host a traditional tea or luncheon at her house, a local restaurant, or a country club. You might also consider an outing to a spa or a day of beauty at a local salon. Everyone gets their nails done while nibbling on sandwiches. A poolside barbecue is often low-key and fun. Or, if your grandmother's up for it (remember: if your luncheon's the weekend of the wedding, all female relatives of both the bride and groom are invited), have a golf tournament of your own.

Your rehearsal dinner gives you yet another opportunity to thank everyone and to shower your guys and girls with some cool gifts. Ties, cuff links, and money clips are all traditional gifts for guys. Jewelry, engraved key chains, and scarves are traditional gifts for girls. But this is also your chance to get creative. I had purses specially designed and filled with fun, wedding-day makeup for each of my bridesmaids. Marie, whose hometown is well known for its pottery, had pottery jars made for their attendants with her and Doug's names and the date of the wedding. Beverly and Chris made CDs for each member of their wedding party with songs that reminded them of each bridesmaid and groomsman (the liner notes included a detailed description of a favorite memory). Choosing gifts for your wedding party is the perfect time to think of each friend's personality and pick a gift to match, something that shows you took some time and effort and manages to say thank you in an extra-special way. Or, if money isn't an object for you, but it is for members of your wedding party, be ultra practical and offer to pay for their wedding-day attire. Nothing says thank you like picking up the tab for a dress or a tuxedo they may never wear again. Plus, it's a really good way to show what a cool friend *you* are.

Mothers and Mothers-in-Law

HANDLE WITH CARE

Mothers. Almost every bride and groom has one, and almost every one of them will start to act just a little bit goofy during the planning of their child's wedding. Imagine: Your child, your precious little baby girl (or boy) just called to say she's getting married. You're thrilled, ecstatic, absolutely head over heels happy for her. You offer to throw an engagement party, immediately make an appointment at the closest bridal salon, and call her every day for a week to see how the plans are coming along. But after that week, you realize you're also a little bit sad (is my little girl all grown up?), scared (am I old enough to be a mother to a grown-up?), and startled (you mean I have to start planning a wedding?). See? There's just something a little complicated about hearing that your child is getting married, which is why your mother and his mother will be thrilled on the inside but may behave rather oddly on the outside. My advice is threefold:

TALK Dive right in and share all the details of your groom's proposal— all the sweet, gushy, intimate things you may be tempted to save for your best friends, but that mothers really want to hear, too. Talk to both your mother and future mother-in-law (steps count, too!) about your initial wedding plans, and be absolutely sure to ask for their advice. Even if your mothers are willing to leave the decision-making to you, they'll be glad you asked.

LISTEN Once you've had your chance to rattle on, it's time to let your mothers rattle on. This may be your wedding, but this is your mother (and his mother) you're talking to, and they may have some ideas of their own. Perhaps an outside spring wedding sounds lovely, but your groom's father has such bad asthma that he might not be able to breathe. If you decide to make the wedding a simple family affair, maybe your mother attended a brunch just the other day and has the perfect spot in mind. Listen to each one's visions of the day, especially to their thoughts on how they'd like to participate. His mother may be thrilled to take over the planning of the rehearsal dinner, while your mother may be more comfortable letting you and a wedding planner take charge of the reception. Listening to your mothers talk about your dream day ensures you understand their dreams and feelings, too.

> Wedding Myth # 14: **Mothers are born knowing how to plan a wedding.** *Yours might or she might not. It's a good idea to get some outside help just in case.*

LEARN One of the nicest things about weddings is the chance you get to learn about your family. There's nothing like the announcement of an engagement to send mothers on a trip down memory lane, recounting their own wedding stories as well as those of relatives you may never even have heard of before (in my family, the legend goes that my great-uncle decided to stand on his head the night before his daughter's wedding). You may also suddenly be inundated with marital advice. In fact, it's an African Lesotho custom for families to gather with the bride and groom before the marriage to "say their piece," sharing their own mistakes and experiences and hopefully sending the couple into marriage wiser than they were themselves. You are going to be filled with a million different emotions before your wedding. How comforting to be able to turn to a mother who has been there herself.

Wedding Myth # 15: **Dads don't count.** *You may be tempted to ignore dear old dad until hitting him up for money as he walks you down the aisle. This is a big day for him, too, so include him in the ceremony and reception plans and all other wedding chatter. (Have your mother hit him up for money.)*

Of course, after all of this talking, listening, and learning, your mothers may still, upon occasion, act a little bizarre, which is how I've gathered so many tales of mother mishaps, misunderstandings, and complete miscommunications from all of my best friends. So, for a little taste of what you may be in for, read on.

MOTHERS WHO DO TOO MUCH

"I purposefully didn't have my wedding in my hometown because I knew my mother would immediately want to take over. She isn't very familiar with San Francisco, so I thought the news (along with our plans to pay for the wedding ourselves) would stop her from trying to run things. Boy, was I wrong. The very next weekend she flew out to help with the planning and every other weekend she was on my doorstep to check on things. It was while we were having a ridiculous fight over the proper way to make a roast beef sandwich that I finally had to sit her down and explain that I wanted my wedding to reflect my new life, who I had become. She took it surprisingly well, flew back home, and was completely low-key during the rest of the planning. And at the wedding, I think she was very proud of me." —LYDIA

MOTHERS WHO DO THE RIGHT THING THE WRONG WAY

"My mother-in-law's heart was completely in the right place. She was thrilled with the news that Billy and I had decided to get married and even more thrilled when we let her know we had decided to turn over most of the wedding planning to her. My mother was in Iowa. Billy's and my work schedules were crazy. His mother was close to the city and more than happy to do all the running around that we couldn't. We told her we wanted our wedding to reflect both our heritages and left her to take care of the details. Which she did with relish, but not without conferring with us about each and every one of them. At least five times a day, Billy and/or I would get a call from his mother: What do you think about this? How would you feel about that? Why don't I send these over so you can look at them? Did I tell you I found this amazing bubble machine? It became maddening and very exhausting. We tried to explain to her that we trusted her judgment, but in the end, it was her excitement and enthusiasm that wound up rubbing off on us. And she was right—the bubble machine was amazing." —SHEA

MOTHERS WHO DO THE WRONG THING THE RIGHT WAY

"Joseph and I were living in New York but the wedding was going to be in my hometown of Tampa, Florida. My mother was more than happy to help out with the planning and was able to reserve the church, reception, and rehearsal dinner sites. She also volunteered to take charge of the invitations and track the responses, which was a huge relief, since we didn't always receive our mail in our basement Brooklyn apartment. Everything went smoothly until we realized at the last minute that without telling us (or the caterer) she had somehow managed to sneak in an extra sixty invitations. The day we were supposed to give the final head count to the reception site, we realized we were going to have to set up extra tables in not one but two side rooms. What a mess!" —BELLA

MOTHERS WHO DON'T DO ANYTHING AT ALL

"Some mothers and daughters just do not get along. I saw my mother once during the whole planning of our wedding—at the actual wedding—which is exactly the way I wanted it." —JANINE

MOTHERS WHO ARE ACTUALLY CRAZY

"I am not going to use my mother-in-law's name, but she is, in fact, crazy. She showed up at all of my prewedding showers completely disheveled. At one, her shoes were mismatched. At another, her hair hadn't even been combed. And at a lingerie shower, in front of all my college friends, my mother, stepmother, and grandmother, she shared explicitly the story of how she first told my groom-to-be about the birds and the bees. And about a week before the wedding, she sent us a letter warning us about marriage and confessing she had never loved her husband (although they were still married) and that, in fact, she was still in love with her high school sweetheart. Apparently, she had had a baby with him, a girl who was still alive somewhere and who she meant to find. We're still not sure if this is true, as she's never mentioned it again." —SUE

Now, your mother may really be crazy. Or, the wedding could simply be making her crazy—which is not far-fetched since weddings are, in fact, crazy. Absolute lunacies, if we're being honest. Your mother may even be making *you* crazy. But here's how I like to think about it: Your wedding is a dream, a dream created by you and your groom-to-be, and dreams, as we all know, are not something that anybody—especially the dreamer—has complete control over. Weird tangents occur. Snags sneak in. Clothes disappear (we've all had *those* dreams). So, know ahead of time that the dream is not going to be perfect. My snag happened to be my hair (I accidentally got it all cut off). My sister's happened to be her dress (she didn't like it). Yours may be your mother. Just remind yourself that you will eventually wake up. The wedding will be over, you will be married, and your mother will either have stopped being crazy, or she will be so far away you won't have to worry about her anymore. You might even count yourself lucky: At least you have a mother, and more important, at least you have hair. Deep down your mother loves you, and you love her, so smile, kiss, and walk down that aisle (with her if you have to). As soon as the wedding of your dreams is over, you can wake up and start living the life you've always dreamed of (well, more or less).

PART II

A Little Before

Vows

YOUR CEREMONY AND YOU

The wedding ceremony is absolutely, positively, without a doubt 100 percent *the* most important part of the wedding day. After all!, this is the part where you actually get married. So why is it that so many couples leave planning the ceremony until the absolute last minute? Well, we brides tend to get a little caught up in things. Things like what style of bouquet to carry—cascade, nosegay, or how about one of those loose lollipop arrangements? What types of photographs to shoot—color, black and white, maybe even a sepia tone? And, of course, the question of what kinds of food to serve—should the vegetarian dish be a pasta with shrimp or that yummy-sounding stuffed eggplant? So were Brian and I ever grateful when we met with our minister to plan our ceremony and he had these wise words to offer: *"Adultery is the atomic bomb of marriage."*

Now, this may seem like a rather strange thing for your minister to be telling you right before your wedding, but for Brian and me, it felt exactly right. Because amid all the talk of food, flowers, photos, and fun that day, our minister's words were one of the only reminders that in a few short months we were not only going to be hosting a wedding, we were going to be getting *married*. And marriages are a serious business. They require commitment, communication, attention, and care. They are also beautiful, bountiful, and bold expressions of love, and our minister spoke eloquently about all of these things.

And the more he spoke, the more we began to realize that while planning a reception for our guests that was relaxed and meaningful was important, planning a wedding ceremony that was relaxed and meaningful was equally as important. In fact, it was more important. Because the wedding ceremony *is* the wedding. It's the occasion for which your family and friends (or even just you and your groom) have gathered, and the spirit present at your ceremony is the spirit that will surround the rest of your wedding day. Your ceremony also symbolizes something a little more private—your marriage and all of the unique and personal values you choose to bring to that marriage. So, after our minister spoke, Brian and I spoke: about our personalities and about all of the ways in which our marriage would be unique. We also explored all of the ways in which marriage could be a tricky business (those atom bombs, for instance).

After all of this talking, we were struck in a way we really hadn't been since the night of our engagement, that we were about to embark on a lifelong journey together. We wanted our ceremony to reflect the vibrant spontaneity and joy of such a moment. We also wanted to honor the solemnity of the moment—our vows before God—and to honor in real and personal ways the family and friends who would be supporting us on our journey. Each part of the ceremony then—the hymns, readings, vows, music—became not haphazard choices to make but real choices to ponder. How did each one contribute to the spirit of the day? How did each one reflect our ties to friends and family? Suddenly, these choices seemed more important than deciding which flowers to carry, photographs to shoot, or foods to serve. And we were going to have to make them quickly, because like all of those other couples, we had waited until the absolute last minute to start planning.

RELIGIOUS CEREMONIES

Before you start flipping through your hymnal or checking out books of poetry from the library, you first need to decide whether to have a religious or a civil ceremony. For many brides and grooms, the decision is easy. Kaye and her groom, James, for instance, both grew up in the Catholic faith, in which marriage is one of the seven sacraments. Kaye's godmother was a nun and helped them pick out a beautiful old cathedral in her hometown of Baton Rouge, Louisiana. She was also very active in helping them plan the ceremony. Kaye says, "Marriages in my family have always been large religious celebrations. My mother's choir sang throughout the ceremony, the priest performed a full mass with communion, and guests filled the cathedral, but having my godmother take part in the ceremony made the experience feel personal and intimate. It was an inspiring way to start our marriage."

The decision was just as easy for Stacey and David, who both grew up in the Jewish faith and are convinced that nothing but a Jewish ceremony would have felt like a real wedding to them. They drafted their *ketubah*, the Jewish marriage contract, together and even now, Stacey admits, if she can't find it, she goes a little nuts. "It really represents to me our wedding and the vows we took not only legally but before God and our families. Plus, you can't get divorced without it, which is something I always tease David about. That contract is a reminder of what we've promised each other—so he better keep those promises, or else."

Finding a religious officiant to perform your ceremony is also sometimes easy. Many couples, once they become engaged, immediately decide to return to the church or synagogue of their childhood because they feel that having an officiant they've grown up with perform their ceremony is a special way of bringing one chapter of their lives to a close as they start another. For some brides and grooms, it's also a comforting way to start a marriage. Their priest or rabbi, rather than being simply a figurehead, is often a friend, and they feel comfortable confiding in him or her their hopes—even their fears—for their marriage. In certain cultures, a religious officiant also serves as a symbol of the bride and groom's community. Weddings are not only about marrying each other but about marrying into a larger community they feel will always be there to support them.

Couples who no longer live near their childhood churches or synagogues but are active in new ones in other cities may find it just as comforting to have their new minister or rabbi perform their ceremony. Anna and Jim, for example, met in college, where they both started attending a local church. The deacon had special services and programs for college students and Anna and Jim found themselves becoming more and more active in the church—and closer and closer to each other. When Jim proposed, they both knew they wanted to have their wedding in their new church. This meant their families would have to travel long distances, but the two felt strongly about having the deacon of their church perform the ceremony. "We had chosen this church and this faith together," Anna says, "and we wanted our ceremony to reflect those choices. It wasn't easy to convince our parents, but it was worth it."

As you look for your officiant, keep in mind that many religions, and even different churches within the same religion, have different rules and restrictions regarding what types of ceremonies they will perform. Some officiants will perform ceremonies only if both the bride and groom are of the same faith, and many have rules particular to their own parish or synagogue. At some Catholic churches, for example, you must be a registered and practicing member of the parish. Couples must make arrangements by calling the rectory at least one year in advance of their intended wedding day and recent (dated no earlier than six months prior to the wedding) copies of baptism and confirmation records are required.

Most religious officiants also require one or more counseling sessions with you and your groom. Brian and I, for instance, met with our

minister twice: once to talk about our ceremony and what it symbolized and once to talk about our marriage and what it meant. In the
Catholic faith these counseling sessions are called Pre-Cana and can
take several months to complete.

Finding an officiant who makes you and your groom feel strong and
more aware of each other as a couple is important. But meetings with
your officiant may not always be fun. After all, he isn't there to help you
plan your wedding, he's there to help you plan your marriage ceremony,
and even more important, your marriage. So while counseling sessions,
or even just talks with your officiant, may not be exactly romantic, they
can be the perfect opportunity for you and your groom to explore your
religion and how it will fit into your future lives together.

CIVIL CEREMONIES

For many couples, planning a civil ceremony is just as perfect. Erin and
Will, for example, are a couple who, although not Buddhist, were interested in incorporating Buddhist elements into their wedding ceremony. They had their astrological charts read and figured out the most
auspicious moment to start the ceremony. But because they didn't belong to a temple, they knew they wouldn't be able to find a Buddhist
priest to perform their ceremony. Through a little bit of research, however, they found a judge who was responsive to their needs. "I think
there's a false notion that just because an officiant is a civil servant he or
she isn't interested in marriages or weddings. A lot of our ceremony
was unfamiliar to our judge, and he was very eager to know the meanings behind each element."

For Serena and Thom, deciding to have a civil ceremony was as
simple as finding a friend. Thom had graduated from law school the
year before and was doing his clerkship with one of the local judges.
The two became very close (Thom even asked for tips for his proposal to
Serena), so when it came time to plan their ceremony, he was the natu-

ral choice. Serena says, "He was also perfect because Thom's Jewish and I'm Catholic. Instead of getting mixed up in the mess of trying to find two religious officiants and making sure none of our family members was offended, it seemed much simpler to have a civil ceremony. And since our judge was a friend, he was able to talk about us as a couple, telling personal stories about us and invoking a familiar tone that I think meant a lot to our families."

Civil ceremonies can also be quick, convenient, and, even when held at a county courthouse, don't necessarily have to be small. Depending on the size of their courtrooms, many courthouses allow couples to invite up to twenty-five guests. Civil ceremonies are also perfect solutions for all of those brides and grooms determined to exchange vows while hang gliding, scuba diving, or throwing themselves through one extreme element or another where their friendly, but not so adventurous, minister may not be quite so eager to follow. And for couples who choose to elope to that itty-bitty, exotic island, a civil officiant may be the person on hand to perform the ceremony.

And, of course, many couples just don't see marriage as a religious commitment: "Our vows and commitment to each other were a completely private matter, for the two of us to decide upon and agree to. The officiant was simply there to make that commitment legal. Marriages come in so many different shapes and sizes—certainly no one religion fits ours." A civil marriage ceremony (despite what your mother may tell you) is perfectly legal; it just comes without all the fuss and fanfare of a religious ceremony—and without any mention of God.

Wedding Myth # 16: **Wedding ceremonies have to be long.** *They can be. But they shouldn't be. Especially if your guests are standing.*

Finding a civil officiant is also generally easier than finding a religious officiant. Check with your city's city hall or your county's marriage license bureau. Also ask friends in the area or your other wedding vendors. For the most part, the only restrictions for a civil ceremony are those required in applying for your marriage license, which makes them the very best types of weddings for couples looking to break the rules.

CREATING YOUR OWN CEREMONY

Of course there are no rules that say you can't mix and match. Many couples come from different religious backgrounds, and even couples of the same religion may find they have different interpretations of their faith. Interreligious ceremonies are very common and many interdenominational and Unitarian ministers can incorporate varying religious traditions. Progressive rabbis and priests also often work together to perform interfaith ceremonies. Or you may choose to hire a civil officiant to preside over your actual marriage vows while a religious officiant is present to appease your parents and to open and close the ceremony with prayer. Creating a ceremony that reflects both your and your groom's beliefs but that doesn't exclude your families and friends can be challenging—but not impossible.

> *Wedding Myth* # 17: **Wedding ceremonies have to be boring.** *Wedding ceremonies can be personal and fun. Kat's niece acted out an excerpt from Peter Pan. Mel and Marco's wedding party gave special readings in English and Italian for their multicultural guests. Joan's and Dave's mothers gave touching testimonials to the couple's love. Love is exciting—your ceremony should be, too.*

Consider the making of Tammy and Awais's wedding ceremony. Awais's family was Muslim. Tammy's was Christian. And although she was planning on converting, she was particularly anxious not to exclude her family or any of her non-Muslim friends from the ceremony.

So, although the couple was in the middle of final college exams and papers, they spent a week in their college's library researching Christian, civil, and Muslim wedding ceremonies. Frustrated, they realized that there wasn't really an official Muslim ceremony, and while their imam, the Muslim spiritual leader who was going to preside over their ceremony, was helpful, he lived in another state and communicating long distance was difficult. Eventually, they came across a Christian missionary's tract on Muslim traditions in Pakistan and this became their guide.

In the end, the couple created a ceremony based on the traditional order of a Christian ceremony but also incorporated Muslim elements: exchanging vows three times, passing out dates to guests, singing selections from the Koran, and exchanging both rings and a Pakistani rug as their *meher*, a kind of reverse dowry in which the groom presents the bride and her family with a gift. "Planning our ceremony," Tammy says, "was definitely a challenge, and it took a lot longer than we expected. But it was really rewarding to be able to include traditions from both our families and to create a ceremony all our own."

The important part about creating your own ceremony is to familiarize yourselves with the ceremonies you are about to break, bend, or mend. The following "Anatomy of a Wedding Ceremony" is the standard order of a traditional wedding ceremony. In civil ceremonies, the religious aspects are taken out, while in some religious ceremonies, many more religious aspects and symbols are often added (communion, scripture readings, the lighting of a unity candle). The wording of each part of the ceremony also differs from religion to religion, so be sure and read the texts from each faith you want to include—and perhaps even from faiths you are simply curious about. Symbols, traditions, even the wording from different religious ceremonies and cultures may strike you and your groom as appropriate for your ceremony. You may also want to add unique elements and symbols of your own creation.

You and your fiancé may even choose to write your own vows, an especially personal and rewarding way to create your own ceremony.

Work closely with your groom and officiant, discussing your feelings about your love and the life you'll be living together and drawing inspiration from scripture, song, poetry, nature, perhaps even your family. Many brides and grooms marrying for the second time who have children promise to love and support not only each other but their families as well. Every marriage is unique, and personalizing your vows is a great way to express what's unique about yours. However, deciding what to include in your vows—or even just your ceremony—will take a little bit of thought on your and your groom's parts as to what your ceremony and vows mean. And I don't mean thinking about these things on your own—I mean thinking and talking about them together.

So pick up a pencil and paper, and as you read through the following description of a ceremony, jot down any ideas and questions (doodles and drawings work, too) you and your groom may have for creating a ceremony that is all your own.

ANATOMY OF A WEDDING CEREMONY

SEATING OF GUESTS Round about the time you are putting the finishing touches on your makeup and your groom is finishing tying (and retying) that bow tie of his, your guests will be taking their seats. An usher or groomsman should be on hand to escort each female guest (if she is with a date, the date simply follows dutifully behind). The escort should also inquire whether your guests would like to be seated on the bride's or groom's side. During this time, guests will have an opportunity to sign the guest book (if there is one); pick up a program (if there is one) and peruse the list of who's who; gaze at the flowers, candles, and other decorations; say hello to the guests they know; introduce themselves to the guests they don't know; and find the package of tissues they've brought along because they know at some point they're going to shed a few tears.

PRELUDE While your guests are busy sitting, signing, and gazing about them, some sort of music should be played. This music, called the wedding prelude, is mainly to let people know they're in the right place but also to set the mood for your wedding ceremony. Perhaps you'd love to hear the sensuous strains of a harp. A series of light and lively Vivaldi violin solos. The dramatic, rhythmic beating of drums, tambourines, and cymbals. Or even simply the sounds of the wind, waves, and the occasional gull as they create their own melody at your ceremony by the sea.

PROCESSIONAL Once your guests have been seated (your makeup finished; his bow tie tied), it's time for the processional. The processional is the part of your ceremony in which you and your groom and all of the people you have chosen to honor (and who have agreed to support you) on this very special day process to the front of the church, temple, courtroom, ballroom, or wherever else you may be having your wedding. Some sort of music should be going on here, too, since walking down an aisle in complete silence while every single one of your guests stares at you can be a little uncomfortable.

The reason, of course, that everyone is staring at you is to check out you and all of your wedding party in your fancy new getups. This can be rather exciting, so don't be surprised if despite any number of rehearsals and lectures your bridesmaids sprint down the aisle, your flower girl refuses to go down the aisle at all, and your dog sprints not only down the aisle but into the laps of all of your guests as well. Not to worry: These mishaps are actually a good thing. For one, it takes a little bit of the attention off your entrance. And two, since there are only a set number of mishaps that can occur during any wedding ceremony, you can be assured that you won't be the one to make them.

Of course, the processional also has some more serious meanings. You and your groom enter separately, from the community of your friends and family, and move toward each other and, if your ceremony is a religious one, into the presence of God. Up until this moment, both of you have been surrounded by dozens and dozens of people, hustle and bustle, noise and nonsense. The processional is all about walking away from this and entering a quiet space to make the most personal and private of commitments. Your friends and family may stand with you in support of this commitment, but their role, for the most part, is a silent one. The processional music dramatizes your journey toward each other, but as you reach the altar or *chuppa,* the music gradually draws to a close and everyone is quiet, observant, and expectant.

OPENING REMARKS Once you and your groom are standing together (eyes shining, hearts pounding, legs quaking), your officiant will begin the ceremony with a few opening remarks. These may be as simple as an acknowledgment of your two witnesses (or in Mike and Machi's case, a grunt and nod toward the closed-circuit camera where the witness to their Vegas wedding was also playing a game of solitaire). Or, your officiant may give a warm and hearty welcome to all eight hundred of your guests, thanking them for their presence and their blessing of the day's very, very important event. He may also offer a prayer to invoke God's presence and blessing as well.

DECLARATION Although not a part of all ceremonies, the declaration is the occasion where you and your groom acknowledge you are entering into marriage of your own free will. The officiant will ask, "Do you take this woman/man to be thy wedded wife/husband?" to which each of you will respond "I do" or "I will." The father or family of the bride is also often addressed with the question "Who presents this woman to be married to this man?" to which your father may respond "I do," "Her mother and I do," or even "Her family does." And since marriage is often seen as a union between your families as well as yourselves, your officiant may address both your and your groom's families—and even perhaps your guests—in a proclamation and response where families and friends agree to support you in your married lives.

At one time, the declaration was also the point in the ceremony when the officiant asked the community if they knew of any reason why the bride and groom should not be married, ending with the rather daunting challenge: "Speak now or forever hold your peace." This is generally left out of most ceremonies today, although some couples enjoy the drama.

EXCHANGE OF VOWS After you and your groom have declared your intentions to each other, your officiant will instruct you to take a couple of steps closer to each other (in Christian ceremonies, the bride and groom also take a couple of steps closer to the altar—and closer to God). Your best lady or attendant takes your bouquet. Your groom takes your hand. And gulp, it's time for those vows, some of the most intimate and meaningful words you and your groom will ever say to each other. You say them once and they bind you in marriage forever. And all of your guests will be there to hear you say them. Obviously, you will want to say all of the right things, skip over the wrong things, speak eloquently, sincerely, with emotion but without being overly sentimental. Your vows should be clear and succinct, not too long, not too short. It's a good sign if your mother suddenly bursts into tears in the middle of them, but a bad sign if you and your groom suddenly burst into tears. If both of you are sobbing, you might be a little difficult to understand, which is a bit of a problem since, as one bride told me, "Your vows are the single most important thing you will ever say in your life."

Wow. This is why many brides and grooms stick to the traditional, tried-and-true, repeat-after-the-officiant type of vows. They are simple, beautiful, real, romantic. And, take my word on this, they will still cause your mother to burst into tears. Bottom line: Traditional vows work. Of course, writing and reciting your own vows can also work. Personal vows are a wonderful way to express your individual feelings for each other and to share your personal promises and hopes for the future. My sister, Shelley, for instance, spoke these simple, beautiful, real, romantic words to her husband, Trevor:

"I take you, Trevor, this day as my husband, and I promise to walk by your side forever, as your best friend, your lover, and your soul mate. May our sunshine be shared, our rains be gentle, and our love eternal. I pledge myself to you from this day forward and for all eternity."

See why guests bring tissues?

Wedding Myth # 18: **Repeating after an officiant guarantees you will get your vows right.** Not necessarily. Jennifer asked Dan to be her wife. April couldn't remember Marty's name. And Leanne couldn't remember her own name. These are important words. If you have to, practice.

EXCHANGE OF RINGS Once you and your groom have exchanged vows (and your guests have shed a few tears), it's time for the exchange of rings. Your groom's best man or the ring bearer fumbles for your ring. Your best lady or ring bearer fumbles for his ring. And with these tender, tender words, you slide your wedding bands onto each other's fingers: "In token and pledge of our constant faith and abiding love, with this ring I thee wed." (At this point, it's perfectly okay to let out a few sniffles yourselves.) Your rings are outward and visible signs of the verbal commitment you have just made to each other and are physical symbols of your union. In religious ceremonies in which an exchange of money or property is required for the marriage, the rings often represent this property. In most religious ceremonies, the rings are also blessed with a prayer to represent your union in the eyes of God.

DECLARATION OF MARRIAGE Yippeee! After the exchange of vows and rings, you and your groom are married, legally, perhaps even in the eyes of God, and your officiant will declare as much with those seven little words you've been dying to hear: "I now pronounce you husband and wife." This is terribly exciting and in many ceremonies is followed by a celebratory song, hymn, reading, or other symbolic act: the lighting of a candle, the drinking of wine, the jumping of a broom. In religious ceremonies, the officiant will also bless the marriage with a prayer, perhaps even inviting your guests to join him in a recitation of the Lord's Prayer. And then it's time for something even more exciting.

KISS The kiss. Oooh, the kiss. The very first one of your married lives, it is a symbol of romantic love, physical love, and your new physical bond. It is also one of the most romantic physical bonds you will ever make. As Brian says, "The kiss is verrrry nice." Practicing the kiss is also verrrry nice, so feel free to do a lot of it. Like right now.

RECESSIONAL Since there's really nothing left to do after that kiss other than smile like a couple of loons, it's time to walk back down the aisle and back into the community of your family and friends, hustle and bustle, noise and nonsense. This is called the recessional, and instead of walking separately, you walk together, bonded by love, law, and, in some cases, God. Of course, to stir up the appropriate level of noise and nonsense you're going to need some more music, which will be your guests' cue to get up from their seats, hunt you down, and hug the stuffing out of you (they might even throw stuff at you). Receive them (and their stuff) joyfully and then all of you can process again—this time to the reception.

A wedding ceremony is exciting. Planning a wedding ceremony is exciting. And planning the rest of your wedding will probably be pretty exciting, too. After all, food and flowers and photographs and dresses and shoes and bands and bow ties and invitations and decorations are all very, very nice. Nice, but not necessary. What is necessary for a wedding is a ceremony (even if it's a simple exchange of vows): a ceremony that is special, meaningful, and personal. A ceremony, in other words, that is all about you.

Caterers*

MINDING YOUR PS AND QS

Picture this: Wedding guests stroll amiably along lush green grounds; gentle breezes lift ladies' hems and softly stir men's slightly loosened ties; ice tinkles in cool drinks as the mother of the bride laughs and the groom shakes hands with the bride's uncle; the groom's father gently pats him on the back before skipping off to grab a plate of BBQ chicken and garlic mashed potatoes.

Beautiful, right? But where in the world is the bride? She's in the kitchen. Honestly, such was the case at a wedding a friend of mine attended recently, and although I hope this was economical, I'm not sure I'd call it a successful wedding. Because a wedding, after all, is about the bride. Yes, yes, it's about family and friends, love and tradition, and all that other stuff, too. At least that's what it's about for you. For everybody else the wedding is about the bride and groom—and most important, the bride. So if no one ever gets to see or congratulate or dance

---

*NOTE: Your caterer may not actually be called a caterer. Yours might be a hotel ballroom manager. Or you may hire a wedding coordinator to handle all of the details from hiring a band to finding your limos while the actual caterer simply prepares and serves the food. Your florist may even act as a kind of party planner, taking care of everything from flowers to linens. But large catering services do everything—one-stop shopping, so to speak—so for the sake of this chapter we're going to call party planners "caterers." They all do the same sorts of things, and they should all have the same sorts of standards. Read on.

with the bride, what's the point? There isn't one. That's why caterers were invented. If you're looking for a casual afternoon cookout, a caterer can do it. An elaborate Mexican fiesta? A caterer can do that, too. A caterer will even work with you on a tight budget. In fact, these days a caterer will do pretty much anything. Think of him or her as your wedding choreographer, the producer of the most fabulous day of your life. Understandably, it's important to choose a caterer who's right for you. And although planning a menu, directing buffet lines, assembling stages and lights, and arranging tables, chairs, flowers, and linens seems like a lot to take care of, finding a caterer to take care of it for you really isn't. Pay attention to these simple guidelines and finding a dream caterer will be as simple as minding your Ps and Qs.

PERSONALITY

First of all, your caterer should have one. A caterer is a people person, a professional party planner, and any caterer you choose should have the personality to match, full of the energy and charisma not only to plan a menu but to host a fabulous reception. Our caterer appeared wearing a comfortably worn denim shirt and seersucker pants. He shook our hands warmly and immediately put us at ease with his slow Southern drawl—the perfect antidote to our harried New York lifestyles. Brian and I had flown to Georgia with visions of planning a typical Southern wedding, and soon after meeting Lee, we were confident we'd found the typical Southern caterer to help us do just that.

This is important, because your caterer's personality should be one you're comfortable with. Different caterers have different styles and your caterer's should match your own. You don't want to hire a caterer who envisions a sit-down dinner for 300 with Dom Perignon and filet mignon when you've been planning on beer and BBQ. While a good caterer will have creative suggestions and visions of his own (ours offered to dress our waiters as drag queens), he should be polite and accommodating when you share your personal wedding vision. Remember, you're paying him money to plan *your* wedding, not his.

Two other personality Ps to remember: patience and pleasure. A good caterer has worked with brides who have dreamed of their weddings since they were five and will tirelessly search for the lace the bride saw in the eighth grade on her favorite soap opera star. On the other hand, every caterer has also worked with brides who have no concept of what they want at their receptions. And while a good caterer will be patient enough to explain your options (a full seven-course meal; an abbreviated, but no less proper, three-course dinner; a dinner buffet complete with pasta, seafood, and stir-fry stations; a casual afternoon tea; or even a breakfast brunch), you should have an idea ahead of time of your particular style and taste. Come prepared to share your wedding dream (even if you just had it last night) with plenty of questions and ideas to help the caterer make your dream come true. You may not know exactly what you want, and a good caterer will help you figure this out, but do have a general sense or you will waste the caterer's (and your) time and possibly end up with a wedding that doesn't suit your taste.

Your reception should reflect both your and your intended's sensibilities—are you black-tie charity ballgoers or backyard ballplayers? You should also take your guests into account. If most of your guests will be family, consider a sit-down family-style dinner, serving large plates of family recipes and swapping age-old family stories and secrets. (Note: If you are having a sit-down dinner for fifty people or more, a seating chart is not optional. It will cause you much pain and suffering, but it is not optional.) If you are inviting a large group of younger guests, consider that food may not be as important as dancing. And if you are having a large reception with both older and younger guests, consider how to balance both groups' interests. Although you may want to focus on the party aspect of your reception and keep the band playing into the wee hours of the night, make sure there are plenty of tables and chairs surrounding the dance floor. Your grandmother may not feel like dancing for three hours, but I'll guarantee she will want to watch. Also, be sure and mix styles of music—you might be surprised by how agile your grandmother is after all.

And lest we forget, planning a wedding is also supposed to be fun, so make sure your caterer is a pleasure to work with. He will be in your life for six months or more and you want the experience to be a good one. This usually means finding a caterer with a good sense of humor. (Ours, for instance, offered to cut us a deal if we found his college-age son an apartment in New York City.) Because even with a good caterer there will be mishaps: It will rain, it will snow, the electricity will cut off in the middle of the macarena. And although your caterer will probably be prepared, he should also—like you—be able to laugh and carry on.

Wedding Myth #19: **Your caterer will be present the day of your wedding.** *Most large catering services host several weddings a weekend. This means your caterer may not attend yours. Ask if your caterer will be present the day of your wedding, and, if not, get the name and telephone number of the head waiter or manager who will be there.*

PRESENTATION

Your caterer could have all the personality in the world, but before you sign him or her up, you should ask to see a presentation. What does the food look like? How is it served? What will the servers be wearing? A good caterer will have a ton of photographs—on the wall, in albums, even scattered loosely around on tables. Because good caterers are (here's another "p" word) proud. They want you to see their work and will describe in detail receptions and events they've held in the past. Our caterer became particularly animated while discussing an African-themed dinner and opera he had helped cater—not exactly what we had in mind for our wedding, but themes are definitely something to consider.

Our wedding reception, for example, was an outdoor Southern wedding, a perfect way to introduce Brian's Philadelphia family to mine. We felt an elegant evening tent wedding would capture my family's traditional Southern style (and please my more formal and traditional relatives), while creating a comfortable and casual atmosphere for two families and separate sets of friends to meet for the first time. Our caterer was particularly excited to meld both North and South, and while showing us his supply of linens, chairs, antique silver urns, and wrought-iron chandeliers, he started talking us through an appropriate menu. We had to have grits, a spicy tomato pudding, and, of course, ham, and sweet potato biscuits, but he would also be open to serving some "Yankee" food. Maybe one layer of our wedding cake could be Italian crème, he suggested. A good caterer will have plenty to offer, providing a variety of ways to match your own particular wedding vision.

Like ours, caterers today can create any kind of theme, complete with appropriate food, decorations, even games. Close friends of mine who also happen to be professional dancers held a beach-side reception complete with oysters, low-country boil, and shag and limbo contests. Caterers will also be able to host culturally inspired weddings, from African to Chinese to Indian. Tammy, for example, searched all over Austin, Texas, before finding a reception site whose caterer would agree to work with an outside caterer to serve both American and Pakistani foods. In general, a good caterer will be excited to accommodate any kind of wedding style you choose, especially if it's something he's never done before.

In addition, a good caterer will not only help you plan your theme, but he will also suggest ways to present it. Your great-grandmother might have gasped at a sit-down dinner that is less than seven courses, but these days a first course, main course, and dessert course are just as acceptable. Don't let your caterer make you feel as if you're committing a faux pas. This is probably a signal he's greedy for your business rather than grateful for it (the more courses you have, the more money he makes). For a simple but just as elegant sit-down dinner, choose a soup and/or salad, a main course with a choice of two or three entrées (beef, chicken, fish, or a vegetable entrée), and a dessert. In addition to your wedding cake, you may serve ice cream, fruit, or a cookie dish at each table. In keeping with Hilary's outdoor wedding in Vermont, at the end of the evening, guests (both the kids and adults) toasted marshmallows over grills and made their own s'mores.

> *Wedding Myth #* 20: ***You and your groom will get to eat any of the food you and your caterer have just picked out.*** Dream on. Have your caterer pack you a picnic basket to go, stay in a hotel with late-night room service, or ask your chauffeur if he'd mind going by the McDonald's drive-thru.

Decide whether guests will preorder via invitations or order at the table during the reception. And if you choose to serve hors d'oeuvres during a cocktail hour before the actual dinner, decide whether you want waiters with trays to mingle among the guests (an option some find a little intrusive) or whether your guests will serve themselves at tables buffet-style. If you choose the latter, make sure the food is accessible and that you have many smaller tables, rather than one large one, to avoid long lines. You might also ask your caterer to set up a few high bar tables without chairs. They're the perfect height for placing drinks while guests mill around, and they can be covered with simple, white linen tablecloths for an elegant look.

If you are having a buffet-style dinner, especially for a large crowd, you should also plan on serving food at several smaller tables. One popular solution is to have different food stations spaced throughout the reception, ensuring that large lines don't form and encouraging guests to mingle. Our wedding reception was held at a historical Southern home, and while we wanted an outdoor tent wedding, we also wanted guests to be able to enjoy and tour the house. Our caterer suggested we set up a bar and a lighter hors d'oeuvres table in the main room of the house, and then set the main buffet dinner tables under the tent, closer to the dance floor. This would encourage guests to wander through the house, but draw people back together again for the dinner hour. If you have a general vision of your reception ahead of time, your caterer will be able to choreograph an enjoyable and successful evening for all of your guests.

If you're having a smaller wedding and don't think you'll be needing a wrought-iron chandelier or a six-foot fountain draped in ivy, a smaller catering service will work just fine. Be aware, however, that smaller caterers often have smaller staffs. They may be able to fix wonderful food, but you may have to hire your own servers or rent your own dishes. At the same wedding reception where the bride was in the kitchen, the groomsmen were directing traffic in the parking lot. In fact, most people were so busy uncorking wine bottles and arranging reception favors that I'm not sure there were any guests at the actual reception!

A larger catering service doesn't necessarily mean you have to have a large wedding. Again, a good caterer offers plenty of choices, for a large or an intimate affair. A larger service simply guarantees that your caterer will be able to provide everything: food, drinks, service, even the flowers if you like. After all, you have plenty of other things to worry about without trying to find plastic spears for your fruit tray. You may want to help plan the menu, but let your caterer decide how to prepare and present it.

> *Wedding Myth* # 21: **Your caterer will automatically know how to get to your reception site.** *Your caterer, along with the rest of your vendors, will need directions to your ceremony and reception sites. They will also need instructions on where to unload and park.*

PRAISE

The best sign of a good caterer is others' referrals. In fact, you may want to choose your reception site first and ask the management which caterers they recommend. Our reception site, for example, had strict rules and guidelines, and only certain businesses are allowed to cater events there. A caterer who is familiar with your site will also be better at planning your event. Our caterer was one of a very short list of people allowed in the house. He had thrown hundreds of parties there and knew exactly how many tables and chairs would fit comfortably in each room. He knew what size tents best fit the front and backyards and knew oh so well the particular quirks of the house's electrical system. A caterer who has worked at your reception site before will have discovered long before your wedding what works and what doesn't.

Praise from previous clients is also a good sign. Ask people from the city where you will be holding your reception about your potential caterer. And if you have friends who have used your caterer, call them up and ask their opinion. That's what friends are for. Note: The higher the caterer's praises, the more popular he'll be, especially during peak wedding seasons. The earlier you look for (and book) your caterer, the better.

Of course all of this does not guarantee your wedding will be perfect, which brings us to the motto of this book: *No wedding is perfect, but every wedding should be fun.* Hiring a perfect caterer ensures that someone else is worrying about the food and all those other annoying details while you are left to have a perfectly good time. Most important, the right caterer will keep you out of the kitchen and in the company of your friends and family.

Those are the Ps of catering. The following are the Qs. Pay close attention and you'll know whether you should hire—or even fire—your prospective caterer.

QUARRELSOME

Your caterer should certainly have a personality, but if he or she is quarrelsome or quick-tempered, it may be time to start searching for another one. Instead of taking the time to listen to your vision for your reception or patiently answering your questions, a quarrelsome caterer will claim he already knows exactly what you want. He will talk over you, even interrupt you, insisting that his linens and decorations will be perfect for your formal function (even if you know from his photographs that you'd like something a little different). "I've done this before," he'll say while planning a menu without taking into consideration the special requests you may have. Although you may feel comfortable leaving most decisions in the hands of your caterer, you should also feel comfortable offering suggestions of your own. This is why it is especially important to come prepared. Have specific ideas, questions, and certainly a vision ready ahead of time. If your caterer tries to manipulate you into having a seven- (or seventeen-) course meal, look at your notes to remind yourself of what your original ideas were. And if your questions and requests make your caterer quick-tempered, move on—quickly.

Tina and Alex, for instance, should have been prepared. They had been discussing their wedding for a year before they were finally able to get engaged. And while their small budget should not have stopped them from planning a reception that was both inexpensive and tasteful, their caterer made them feel as if they couldn't afford anything more than the most basic decorations and favors. He demanded they trust his creativity, and sadly, they wound up with a wedding that was neither their taste nor anyone else's they knew. The lesson: Beware of a caterer who is a fast talker, quick to take your money, and then hurries you out the door.

QUOTE

The most obvious way to tell a good caterer from a bad caterer is by his or her quote. A professional caterer will quote prices up front and draw up a proposal detailing all charges for food, drinks, lighting and decorations, and service. He will talk candidly about setup and cleanup fees and make sure you understand exactly what it is that you're paying for. If your quote doesn't include certain items, ask about them, and if your caterer is tight-lipped (i.e., quiet) about quoting you prices or refuses to put quotes on paper, hunt for someone a bit more straightforward.

Also make sure your caterer's quote is for the correct number of people attending your reception. Courtney's caterer quoted her a price based on 100 people even though she was having 150 guests. The great price turned out not to be so great after all. "If it seems too good to be true," she said, "it probably is." Don't assume your caterer is giving you a good deal. Make sure he lays not only the food, but also the prices, out on the table. And be sure and ask specific questions until you feel confident you are getting a fair price. A good caterer will negotiate with you; a bad one will quibble.

QUESTIONABLE REFERENCES

One of the most important requirements is that your prospective caterer is a complete professional and has the proper catering credentials. Make sure he or she has all the necessary health permits and is insured for liability. For example, if you are serving alcohol, confirm that he has the proper license. Some caterers may be able to serve alcohol, but may not be allowed to purchase it. If this is the case, arrange to buy the alcohol yourself a few days before the wedding and have it delivered to the caterer. Your caterer or local package store should be able to give you guidelines for purchasing the appropriate amount of alcohol for your size reception.

If your caterer does purchase the alcohol for you, ask how you will be charged. Many caterers will charge per drink. Others may charge per bottle. Others might charge you for only what your guests consume— a nice option if you're concerned that you will have bottles of wine and liquor left over. Know ahead of time whether your guests are heavy or light drinkers and your caterer will help you decide which option is best for you. A really good caterer will even know which alcohols will be most popular at your reception. Because our wedding was in June, typically a rather warm season, our caterer recommended serving white liquors and white wines rather than darker liquors and red wines that are more popular during the fall and winter seasons.

And even if your caterer seems completely charming, it's always a good idea to ask for references, a lesson Shirley learned the hard way. "The owner of the bed and breakfast where we had our wedding seemed perfect. She called everybody 'dear' and 'darling' and claimed to have once been a model in New York. And she offered to take care of everything, from the rehearsal dinner to the ceremony to the reception. Well, the entire event was a disaster: The owner showed up drunk, the flowers were dead, the cake was crooked, the food was absolutely terrible, and there wasn't any music. All of our guests had to hum 'Hear Comes the Bride' as I came down the aisle. A little research would have saved us a lot of heartache."

The staff at your reception site should also be able to recommend good caterers and can match your type of reception with the most appropriate vendor. While searching for other wedding vendors—your photographer, band, or florist—ask for their recommendations for caterers as well. Good caterers develop reputations not only through pleased clients, but also through the other businesses they work with.

Counting the Ps and Qs in this chapter isn't necessary, of course, but you will want to mind them, because the more Ps your caterer has, the better he'll be at planning the perfect wedding of your dreams. The fewer Qs he has means the fewer chances that you'll hire a quacky caterer with questionable quirks who will up and quit on you.

Cake

HIS AND HERS

At one of the very first weddings I ever remember going to, I was sick. I had a fever of 103 degrees and it wasn't safe to eat or drink anything other than crackers or ginger ale. However, once I walked into the reception and my five-year-old eyes spied that magnificent, white, three-tiered creation called a wedding cake, it was love at first sight. My mother, noting my wide eyes a bit fearfully, offered me a deal: I could either have a slice of the wedding cake, or, if I waited until I was well, she would make me a whole strawberry cake of my very own. Tempting. Really. I thought this over for at least a full second before skipping over to the cake table. With visions of those icing roses dancing in my head, I received my first slice of wedding cake with something akin to awe and carried my plate away from the crowd so I could savor it by myself.

Then came my first bite. Slowly, tears ran down my face. The cake was terrible, one of the worst things I had ever tasted. Even the icing roses tasted horrible. Incredulous, I quietly made my way to the other side of the room and threw the rest of the cake into a trash can. I felt cheated and very, very sad as I stood in line for a glass of ginger ale.

Now, wedding cakes can be magnificent, white, three-tiered creations. Wedding cakes can also be whimsical, romantic, funny, inspiring, short, tall, or sweet. But please (please), a wedding cake should never, ever be sour. Take the time to choose a baker carefully. Many caterers work directly with a specific baker, in which case, choose your caterer carefully. Ask to see photographs and samples of the baker's designs and also arrange for a cake tasting. Brian and I sampled about five different kinds of cake and twice as many bowls of icing before deciding on an absolutely delicious white velvet raspberry and Italian crème combination. We then presented our baker with a picture of a cake we'd fallen in love with in a magazine and had her copy it exactly—a simple but striking three-tiered cake with whipped white icing and red rose petals scattered around each layer. This striking cake just happened to be made by the very best baker in town. How do I know? Because everyone in town told me so.

Ask around and find out whose cakes are out of this world and schedule a meeting immediately. Talk openly to your baker about your likes, dislikes, the rest of your menu, the style of your dress, the design of your invitation, and any unique motif you're incorporating into the wedding. Ask questions: Will she only make her own designs, or is she open to suggestions? Will she work to create the perfect cake for you and your groom-to-be, perhaps even providing sketches? Amy and Brian's wedding cake design, for example, incorporated shamrocks from his family's roots in Ireland and bundles of wheat from her family's roots in Iowa. Staci, who is absolutely crazy about the color purple, had her white cake decorated with dozens of cascading purple icing roses. And Nelly, whose theme for the wedding was pearls, had her cake decorated with tiny seedlike pearls of icing. The cake was set between two candelabras draped with ivy, and each pearl, she remembers, seemed to glow. But her favorite part of the cake? Each of the four layers was a completely different (and completely yummy) flavor.

You will also want to talk openly to your baker about your budget. If you'll be inviting 150 guests but aren't sure you can afford that fabulous three-tiered creation, let her know. She may be able to create your dream rose-covered cake on a smaller scale and serve a less expensive (but equally as tasty) white sheet cake from the kitchen. Also ask if serving cakes beside each other on different-size pedestals, or even stacked directly on top of each other rather than on tiers, will save you money. Often, the process of stacking cakes on tiered platforms is tricky and time-consuming, and therefore more expensive. Or, have your mother or grandmother whip up your favorite strawberry cake. Just be sure and ask your caterer or banquet hall manager if your reception site allows outside cakes and if there's a serving fee (sometimes called a fork fee).

Also be sure that someone takes great, great care transporting your dream cake to the reception. Ask ahead of time if your baker delivers. Many large bakeries do, but some smaller businesses do not. If yours doesn't, don't leave this task up to Dad. Wedding cakes are very, very fragile and, so I've heard, actually enjoy falling completely apart right before weddings. Arrange for a skilled delivery person, perhaps even with your baker or baker's assistant, to deliver the cake to your reception site—and make sure your cake table is sturdy. At Teresa and Lee's wedding, their elaborate six-foot wedding cake went flying through the air when one of the table legs collapsed. Cake and frosting landed on nearby guests and Teresa's mother spent the rest of the reception crying.

Wedding Myth # 22: **Your groom will not smoosh wedding cake in your face**. *He's a boy. Consider yourself warned.*

If your cake is being driven a long distance, make especially sure the cake, as well as the passengers, are up for the trip. Jeannette and Todd's wedding cake, a present from Todd's aunt, survived the first hour of the drive to Florida without incident. The second hour, however, the air conditioner shut off and everyone—plus the cake—started sweating. Todd's ten-year-old cousin, John, the first to notice the dripping icing, had an inspired idea of how to clean up the mess—with his fingers. By the time they arrived at the wedding, Todd said he wasn't sure which was the cake and which was his cousin. John, however, has no regrets. "It was good," he said.

Another "good" idea is to ask your baker which kinds of cake and icings are appropriate for the time of year of your wedding. The day of our outside wedding threatened to be particularly hot and our caterer recommended keeping the cake inside the house to protect the icing from the sun. We compromised by keeping the cake inside for most of the reception and then bringing it out onto the front porch for the cake cutting.

And then, of course, there's the groom's cake. The groom's cake is one of those silly Southern traditions that somehow wound up migrating north, west, and anywhere people want to have a little fun. These cakes are designed either by or for the groom in the shape of the groom's hobby or favorite pastime. Chris, an avid fly fisherman, had his cake made in the shape of a trout. Dan, who had just graduated from the police academy, had a cake in the shape of a police badge. Brian's cake (a surprise planned by yours truly) was a replica of his favorite board game, Flick-A-Nik. Grooms' cakes are generally rich chocolate creations made to balance the white wedding cake, but feel free to throw tradition to the wind. Tony had his heart set on his absolute favorite dessert: turtle pie. And in England, the groom's cake is often a fruitcake. You might choose to serve the groom's cake alongside the traditional wedding cake or box up slices for guests to take home (ask if your baker or caterer will provide cake-slice boxes). Legend has it that any single woman who sleeps with the slice of the groom's cake under her pillow that night will dream of her future husband.

Your groom's cake and/or wedding cake doesn't even necessarily have to be made from cake. Consider the couple who was having a 7 A.M. wedding at a restored dairy barn in South Carolina. They knew a traditional wedding cake somehow didn't seem appropriate, but were unsure of what else to serve. Suddenly, they both recalled one of their favorite breakfast treats—Cinnabons. Before they knew it, they were calling the Cinnabon company in Atlanta, Georgia, to see if they could possibly make a Cinnabon wedding cake. Cinnabon's answer: Why not? Not only would Cinnabon make the wedding cake, they'd donate it to the lucky couple. Two hundred Cinnabons were stuck together to form three layers and smothered in white icing. On the outside it looked just like a wedding cake; on the inside it was pure Cinnabon. Voilà—the perfect breakfast wedding cake.

For many brides and grooms, sometimes cake just isn't enough. Feel free to load up your tables with cookies, candies, fruits, and pastries. Serve a sorbet during dinner and an assortment of pastries with coffee. One bride whose wedding lasted into the wee hours of the morning had her caterer set up a crêpe station where guests could choose their own fillings. I've even heard of couples setting up sundae bars. Or, consider a kid-friendly treat such as a plate of Rice Krispies Treats. Nancy says, "There's never an occasion that goes by in our family where someone doesn't bring the Rice Krispies Treats, and our wedding was no exception."

Desserts of any kind, and especially your wedding cake, can be wonderful expressions of your and your groom's personalities, cultures, and traditions. They do not have to be especially big. They do not have to be especially elaborate. But they should be especially good. So, like I said earlier, choose your baker (or caterer or recipe) carefully. Otherwise, you run the risk of making some bright-eyed little girl very, very sad.

Music

BANDS, DJS, AND ALL THAT JAZZ

Whoever heard of a wedding without music? Certainly not Brian and me, who are already huge fans of music anyway. That's why when it came time to planning our wedding, we knew we were going to have to have some music. What kinds? All kinds. A violin and organ for our prelude, processional, and recessional, a couple of special hymns for guests to sing during the ceremony, and a live band to get everyone out on the black-and-white checkerboard dance floor at our reception. We even invited a few friends to bring along their guitars and banjos to keep things cookin' while the band took their break. Music, in our humble opinions, is one of the single most wonderful things in the world. It ranks right up there with love, which is why on a day so filled with love we also wanted to fill it with music.

So, for two people who love music, picking out music and musicians was easy, right? Wrong. It wasn't easy at all and here's why. Musicians are tricky. They will try and make you think they can do all sorts of things that they really can't. Why? Because all musicians (even DJs, who aren't really musicians but wish they were) really, really want you to hire them. Just because they want you to hire them, however, doesn't mean that you should. With that in mind, the following is a guide to all different kinds of musicians, the tricks they typically play, and why hiring a band, a DJ, a string quartet, or even a tuba player has nothing whatsoever to do with what they *say* they can and can't do—and absolutely everything to do with what their music actually *sounds* like.

CEREMONY MUSICIANS

Music is one of those little details that can make your wedding ceremony unique and special. Think ethnic: Michelle and Michael hired a group of traditional Spanish musicians to serenade guests as they arrived at their garden wedding. Religious: Audrey and Daryl had their church's gospel choir perform the Lord's Prayer after their exchange of vows. Personal: Chris, a jazz pianist, surprised his bride by playing an original composition for her as she walked (in shock) down the aisle. Your music, more than any other single element, brings your personal vision for your wedding to life. Music sets a tone, a certain atmosphere, and communicates in a way that flowers and dresses and even words can't: "Here we are, let's get married!"

Like I said earlier, there are all kinds of music. There are also all kinds of musicians. And the first step in choosing either is to consider which ones are right for you and your ceremony. An organ, for example, with its regal, resounding notes, its pomp and grandeur, and its large, loud, and lovely sound, is sure to strike up a bit of commotion—and emotion—at your wedding ceremony. It sets the appropriate mood for a formal church affair and is the perfect choice for your dramatic entrance to Mouret's Suite no. 1, Rondeau (*Masterpiece Theater*), or Wagner's bridal chorus ("Here Comes the Bride"), for instance. Hint: An organ is guaranteed to get everybody's attention.

A piano can be just as grand (Beethoven's "Ode to Joy" from his Ninth Symphony is a spectacular piano recessional piece) but is also a bit more versatile. Instead of classical, think contemporary: Gershwin, George Winston, a love song from your favorite Broadway musical, or the theme song from your favorite movie. Soft and sweet, a piano creates an intimate and romantic atmosphere. But by no means does your piano have to be timid—or even traditional. If sappy ballads make you snore, why not pick something a bit funkier, like James Brown's "I Feel Good," to accompany *his* walk to the altar? Or the oldie but goody, "Ain't We Got Fun?" to get you both boogying back down the aisle?

Of course, you may want to hire other musicians and singers instead of—or in addition to—your pianist and organist. That tuba player, for instance. Or a string quartet, a woodwind ensemble, a flute choir. A harpist, a violinist. A trumpet player, a guitar player, a sitar player. Flute, lute, mandolin, harpsichord. A voice solo, a duet, an entire choir. One of each isn't necessary, of course (you're planning a wedding, not a music festival), but a combination of several can be delightful. So how do you find the perfect music and musicians? You look, and even more important, you listen.

Where the Musicians Are

If you're holding your ceremony in a house of worship, you will most likely be given the name of an in-house pianist, organist, or even a music director. This person is responsible for helping you coordinate the music for your ceremony and will either be available to play at your wedding herself or will refer you to a list of other in-house piano and organ players. Many churches and temples have musicians on staff (instrumentalists as well as vocalists) or regularly use soloists and ensembles from the community. Your music director may work closely with the director of another community music program (a community orchestra, chorus, or college music program) and should be able to suggest talented and appropriate musicians for your ceremony. You may also be able to hire your church or temple choir, an expensive but especially grand way to celebrate such a special day. However, before considering any musicians, be sure and ask your music director for suggestions as to what types of music work best at your site. While a cello and acoustic guitar duo may be the perfect choice for that small chapel on the hill, you may need something a little bolder to fill up the cathedral whose ceilings reach almost to heaven itself.

---

*Wedding Myth # 23: **The louder the music, the better.** Your musicians are playing music to accompany your ceremony, not to compete with your ceremony. Make sure all microphones and speakers are set to the appropriate volume.*

If your ceremony is at a site other than a house of worship, or if your site doesn't have a music director, you might still want to call a local church or temple in the area for references (many pianists and organists are available to play at sites other than their houses of worship). Or, feel free to contact the directors of local music programs yourself. College music programs are an especially good source of musicians, since many students help put themselves through college by playing at weddings and can be a less expensive—but just as beautiful—alternative to professional musicians.

References from friends are always a good idea, although I'd beware of hiring a musician based solely on a friend's suggestion. Music tastes range widely, and the violin your friend calls "angelic" you may call "demonic." If at all possible, arrange to hear your musicians in person, privately or while they perform at another event—or at least ask for a tape. This is especially important when choosing specific pieces of music for your ceremony. Songs you may have heard on a CD or radio program are often backed by an entire orchestra, which (unless you're very, very lucky) probably won't be putting in an appearance on your wedding day. And if you'll be using a tape or CD player at your ceremony or reception, make sure each song is already cued before you press play.

What the Rules Are

Rules? Yep, unfortunately, most ceremony sites do have certain rules when it comes to music. Many churches, for example, restrict the types of music that may be played during a wedding ceremony. Some Catholic churches prohibit the bridal chorus from Wagner's *Lohengrin* and the wedding march from Mendelssohn's *A Midsummer Night's Dream* because they're considered secular music, and many rabbis prohibit both as well since Wagner was a well-known anti-Semite and Mendelssohn converted to Catholicism. Other churches may restrict your music to classical pieces (read: no Top 40 countdown) and many will allow only live music to be performed (read: no boom boxes). Orthodox Jewish and Quaker ceremonies forbid music altogether. Before hiring any musician or choosing any piece of music, be sure to get your music director's or officiant's permission.

Other ceremony sites may have restrictions regarding your use of music as well (especially when it comes to your reception music). Check with your site's coordinator for specific rules on what types of music and instruments are allowed. Many historical sites restrict music to lighter instruments: flute, violin, piano. Larger and louder instruments (trumpet, kettle drum, electric guitar) may cause damage to antiques in the site and are strictly forbidden (such loud music in small spaces may also cause damage to your guests' eardrums, so don't think of this rule as a bad thing).

If your ceremony is being held outside, you may need to register for a music/sound permit, and again, expect certain restrictions. Depending on the location of your site, many communities have rules regarding the types of music and musicians that are allowed in public spaces, the noise level of your musicians, the time of day of your event, and the length of your event. An outside site may also pose its own natural physical limitations. Will your musicians need a stage or other platform? Is there a cover in case of rain? Do your musicians need outlets for microphones or other electrical equipment? Before setting your heart on a site—or musician—make sure that your musician will actually be able to perform at your site.

Listening to Your Musicians

Most important, make sure your musicians can perform, period. If you're working with your site's music director and have heard her play before, a simple phone call to reserve her services will suffice. As your wedding date grows closer, you can set up a meeting to pick out your actual ceremony music: prelude, processional, solos, hymns, recessional. If you'd like to hire additional musicians to perform at your ceremony, your music director should be able to offer suggestions and even arrange a time for you to hear a few musicians perform. However, if time is limited, you may want to take your music director's word that the violinist she's recommended is both talented and reliable.

On the other hand, if your ceremony site doesn't have a music director and you've never heard any of your potential musicians perform before, set up a meeting immediately. While talking over possible processional and prelude tunes, have them play each selection for you. This is your chance to figure out what songs you like and to hear whether or not your musicians can actually play. Just because someone is your chapel's organist doesn't mean she can play the organ well. And there's nothing like a bad note or two (or twenty) to ruin your walk down the aisle, which is why I've put together the following.

Tricks Ceremony Musicians Play

Most of the instrumentalists and vocalists you will come across while planning your wedding are accomplished musicians. They will play and sing nothing but beautiful music on this once-in-a-lifetime, beautiful day. Unfortunately, some musicians can be rather sneaky. More than a couple of brides I've talked to wound up being more impressed with the tricks their pianists played than the music they played (or didn't play). So, just to prepare you, I've listed some of the most common ploys your musicians may use:

PRETEND THEY CAN PLAY Like I said earlier, just because someone is an organist doesn't mean he or she can play the organ well. Arrange to hear your musicians play before your wedding day, especially if you're considering asking a friend to play or sing at your wedding. Flattered and eager to please you, most friends will say yes, skipping over the very important fact that playing in public has been known to give them a serious case of the hiccups. If you've only really heard your roommate sing in the shower, chances are there's a reason.

PRETEND THEY CAN PLAY YOUR REQUESTS Pride. All musicians have it, which is why even if they're not familiar with a piece of music you've requested, they'll often claim they are. If you're nervous your pianist may just be pretending to know Tesla's "Love Song," ask her if she'd like you to buy her the sheet music, and then arrange a time to hear her play through all of your selections. Tell her music is very important to you and you're trying to get a full picture of what your wedding day is going to sound like.

PRETEND THEY'RE AVAILABLE All musicians want to be hired—therefore no musician will ever say they're not available. Unfortunately, sometimes they're not (or they double-book) and will send a replacement to sit in for them at your wedding. This may be a less accomplished player (who hasn't practiced your music selections), and at one bride's wedding turned out to be a pianist's music student. Amateur, as well as professional, ensembles also have a habit of substituting players. Confirm ahead of time the exact names of the musicians who will be playing on your wedding day.

PRETEND THEY'LL BE ON TIME Your musicians may actually be available on your wedding day—but that doesn't mean they'll be on time to the wedding. Confirm all dates, times, and directions a day or two before the wedding, and if your musicians still seem confused, have someone call each one the actual day of the wedding. If you ruffle any feathers, you can always blame it on being a nervous bride (a neat little trick of your own).

RECEPTION MUSICIANS

Finding musicians for a small reception can be a lot like finding musicians for your ceremony, especially if your reception is a quiet afternoon lunch or a simple evening gathering for cake and champagne. Reception musicians play all the same roles ceremony musicians do. They can be dramatic: a Moroccan ensemble complete with a belly dancer. Romantic: a couple of strolling violinists. Lovely: a harp and woodwind ensemble. Lively: a barbershop quartet. Or just plain fun: a free jukebox filled with Golden Oldies. Just because your reception is small doesn't mean you can't be creative.

Larger receptions, however, are a different story entirely. More guests equals more noise, and the louder your guests are going to be, the louder your music needs to be—especially if you want to get people dancing. This usually means one of three things: hiring a band, a DJ, or a combination of both. As you consider these three options, keep in mind that large receptions are usually comprised of several smaller events: a cocktail hour, the bride and groom's entrance, the bride and groom's first dance, the father-daughter dance, the mother-son dance, the champagne toast, the cutting of the cake, dinner, the bouquet toss. You'll want the appropriate music—and musicians—to accompany each event. Music sets a certain mood. It also creates a certain tempo: slow while you're eating; fast while you're dancing; faster still while you're running for that getaway car. And because you certainly won't be paying attention to what tempo's appropriate when, you'll need a band or a DJ that will.

*Wedding Myth # 24: **All love songs are appropriate first
dance songs.** Guess again. For instance, "Every Breath You
Take" by Sting is not about a smitten lover. It's about a stalker.
"With or Without You" by U2 is ultimately about not being able
to live with your love. And "I Will Always Love You" by Whitney
Houston is a very sad song about a woman who has lost her
love. Tip: Listen closely to the words of any special song you
pick out.*

You may even want your band leader or DJ to act as emcee for the
evening, announcing your entrance, the arrival of each dinner course,
and working in tandem with your wedding director or site coordinator
to cue your guests (and you) when it's time for each event. Obviously,
then, you'll need a band or a DJ that's familiar enough with weddings to
understand the pacing of a reception—and one that's prepared. After all,
weddings can get kooky: tables topple, cakes collapse, and mothers,
well, mothers cry. And through it all, your band or DJ should be able to
keep calm, keep up, and, more important, keep the music playing.

Bands

Live bands can be a lot of fun. Brian and I had a live band at our reception that people are still talking about. Or rather, they're still talking about our band's lead singer, who, dressed to the nines in a fabulous
red sequined dress, sang her heart out and shimmied around on stage
with dance moves I'm not sure some of our guests were ready for. Our
bass player was just as funky, with a mean, low-thumpin' guitar and a
voice to match. And the rest of the band, with their drums, horns, guitars, and vocals, was so full of energy, I think even they were sorry to see
the wedding end.

Finding a good live band, however, can be tricky and is often expensive. Bands can cost from $1,000 to $4,000 and three times as

much in major cities. So, as you start the search for the perfect wedding band, realize it can take some time—and some money. Look back at your wedding plan and think about how important a live band actually is for your reception. For Brian and me, a band was always a must-have. After such an exciting event as getting married, we wanted to celebrate—i.e., dance. Hence, we took a little money from our flower budget and put it into the band budget. However, if you know dancing isn't exactly your guests' kind of thing, you may want to look for a smaller ensemble to accompany your dinner party, or simply go with a DJ. But for getting a party started, keeping a party going, and getting and keeping your guests on the dance floor, there's nothing better than good, live music from a good, live band.

Where the Bands Are

The first thing to know about bands is that there are all kinds of them: Dixie, swing, big band, beach, Latin, country, jazz, reggae, calypso, rock, disco, blues. Take a look at your reception site, your guest list, and your wedding vision and play a little game of match. Calypso on the beach. Country on the farm. Jazz on the city rooftop deck. Or you could hire one of those all-purpose bands that plays a little bit of everything. These bands will provide a list of the types of music they play—big band, oldies, jazz, Top 40, etc.—letting you decide which are appropriate for your reception. Most will also provide you with a song list, giving you an even better idea of the variety of music they can play.

So where do you start looking for a band? First, ask your friends. Most of us, by this time in our lives, have heard a ton of wedding bands and are full of advice for getting people on the dance floor and may even be able to suggest a specific band. Your caterer or site manager will also have suggestions. Or, contact an entertainment company that represents bands, DJs, and other entertainers in your area. Entertainment companies are listed in the telephone book and often post advertisements in local wedding magazines. With a simple phone call, you'll be put in contact with a manager who will ask for the details of your wedding. Based on your description, he or she will be able to recommend several different bands and put together packages of tapes, videos, and press materials for each one. It's your job to sift through the packages and decide which band's right for you.

Local fraternity, college, or community organization social councils are also great places to search for a band. All regularly throw parties for various types of events and themes (reggae, beach, rock) and will be able to suggest bands appropriate for your reception. After having struck out with friends' suggestions and our caterer's referral, I called the entertainment coordinator at my former college in Atlanta and was lucky enough to snag the amazingly talented "Total Package" (red dress and all) for our wedding day.

Listening to Your Band

If you can arrange to hear a potential band in person, go, go, go. There's nothing like hearing a band live to check out their sound, style, and a little something I call sensitivity training. Are they quiet and low-key, subtly cueing guests when it's time for dinner? Are they upbeat and talkative, leading guests in line dances and inviting guests onstage? Do they invite themselves offstage and onto the dance floor—during the bride's and groom's first dance? If you and your groom have popped in on a wedding that you haven't been invited to, you're not going to want to meet and greet or mix and mingle, of course. But you will want to stay long enough to get a sense of the band's song list and how the other guests respond to the music and whoever's on the mike.

However, for brides doing the long-distance thing, sadly, you're going to have to rely on tapes and videotapes. This means suffering through some really bad music and some really (really) bad sales pitches. The most entertaining pitch I had to endure came from a super-smooth, super-fast-talking Southerner who promised a one-of-a-kind party band with male and female vocals surpassing the theaters of London and Broadway. While the band was definitely one of a kind (they're the only band we considered who offered to perform original rap songs while dressed in Egyptian outfits), their vocals were more like "Bring in Da Noise"—without the "Funk." Even with all of the video's special effects—fade-ins, fade-outs, freeze-frames, and slo-mo sequences—we were not impressed. Hint: While watching your potential band's video and/or listening to their tapes, you're listening for music, not too-good-to-be-true testimonials or special effects. While you may be looking for a lively band leader to get all of your guests on the dance floor, you'll also want to make sure the band can play the music to match.

Tricks Bands Play

More than any other types of musicians, bands want you to hire them. And it's not just because they need the money. It's also because they really like to play, which is why some bands will do absolutely anything to make you think they can play—and do all sorts of other things they probably can't. Here are some of their most common tricks:

PRETEND THEY'RE VERSATILE Any band will pretty much promise to be anything you want it to be. But here's a hint: A country band that only knows "Achy Breaky Heart" and "I've Got Friends in Low Places" is not a country band. If you're looking for a specific style of band (swing, jazz, country), a good band will be able to play a variety of tunes in that style for the duration of your reception (usually around four to five hours). Similarly, if you're hiring an all-purpose band with the idea that you'd like to hear a variety of styles of music throughout the evening, your band should be able to play all of those styles. Check your band's song list carefully, making sure you like their variety of songs, and then check the band's tape or video carefully, making sure they can actually play each song.

PRETEND THEY'RE *NOT* AVAILABLE I know, this seems completely counter to what I said about musicians wanting to be hired. They do, which is why they'll often say they're not sure if they're available, that their calendar seems to be filling up quickly that month, that they'll have to check and let you know. This is all supposed to make you panic and reserve their services right away. *Your* trick is to go ahead and reserve their services right away, delay on sending the deposit check, and then if you find a better band, cancel. Trust me, if the band's good, someone else will hire them.

PRETEND THEY HAVE THE EQUIPMENT THEY NEED Some bands will pretend to have all the equipment they need to play at your reception site—up until about three days before your reception. If you want to avoid a wild-goose chase around your not-so-small town looking for a generator or an extension chord or an amp or some other piece of equipment you've never heard of, make sure your band's manager talks to your reception site's manager and works out all of these details way before the wedding day. All reception sites have different musical requirements and it's your band's job to know them, not yours.

DJ♦

A DJ can also be a wonderful choice for your reception. For one thing, hiring a DJ for your wedding reception guarantees that your song requests will actually sound like the songs you requested (which means your guests will actually be able to dance to them). And forget being tricky, DJs really are versatile, capable of switching from jazz to rock to country to disco with the simple change of a CD. DJs are also good choices for smaller reception sites where the sounds of a full band may be a bit overwhelming. Lindsay and Rob, for example, had always thought they'd hire a band for their 150-guest wedding, until they visited their reception site while a reception was in progress: "As soon as we walked into the restaurant, we cringed. The acoustics were so terrible the band just wound up sounding like a bunch of noise. We immediately knew we'd have to hire a DJ." And fear not, a good DJ can pack the dance floor (or provide the perfect background music) just as well as a live band. DJs are also less expensive and aren't all that difficult to find.

Wedding Myth # 25: **Bands and DJs can read your mind.** *If you are opposed to "YMCA," "Celebration," "We Are Family," "The Electric Slide," the macarena, the chicken dance, the bunny hop, the hokey pokey, or any variation thereof, now is the time to say so.*

Where the DJs Are

Good DJs can be found in all of the same places wedding bands can. Start by asking friends for suggestions and checking with your reception-site manager or caterer for referrals. Many caterers have a list of DJs they work with regularly and will be able to recommend one that matches your tastes and budget. Entertainment companies are also good sources for DJs. Describe the size, style, and budget of your wedding to a manager, as well as the age range of your guest list, and he should be able to suggest a DJ appropriate for your reception's level of formality who can cater to the musical tastes of all your guests: your niece Emily *and* her namesake, great-aunt Emily. You might also consider calling local clubs and radio stations and asking for the names of DJs who work at weddings. Club and radio disc jockeys often come with top-of-the-line equipment and built-in libraries of almost every style of music imaginable. Their fees, however, may be quite a bit higher. The key is to shop around until you find the DJ whose style and price is right for you.

Listening to Your DJ

Just because your DJ isn't a musician doesn't mean you shouldn't arrange to listen to him or her perform. Different DJs have different styles and musical tastes and you'll want to make sure you choose a DJ whose style and taste match your own. Is he upbeat and friendly, graciously taking guests' requests? Or is she rude and crude, more of a "shock jock" than a "hostess with the mostest"? Is his idea of slow music your idea of slow music? Does her idea of fast music get your toes tappin'? And can she mix and match the fast music with the slow music without skipping a beat? A wedding, after all, is made up of lots of different tempos and lots of different moments: your entrance, your exit, your first waltz, your last tango. And your DJ is responsible for putting together the music for all of these. In other words, he's in charge of putting together the soundtrack for your wedding. So before you hire someone to set this special day to music, make sure you find a DJ who understands what you want the day to sound like.

This means arranging a meeting with your DJ (in person or over the phone) to discuss your wedding vision candidly. If you absolutely do not want your DJ to talk, ask him if this is a problem. Or, if you'd like your DJ to act as the master of ceremonies for the reception, announcing your and your groom's entrance and other events throughout the evening, ask if he's worked at a wedding before and if he feels comfortable with spinning *and* talking. Work out details such as whether he'll take requests from guests (and what to say if you really don't want him to). And don't forget to give him a complete schedule of the evening's events: your entrance, approximate times for toasts (be sure to include how many: best man, father of the bride, etc.), and approximate times for the cutting of the cake, tossing of the bouquet, and, most important, your exit. A good DJ will want to get an idea of the atmosphere you're trying to create as well as the pace of your reception before putting together an appropriate song list.

You should also give your DJ your own song list, beginning with any "must-have" songs: your first dance, the father-daughter dance, the hora, your mother and father's first-dance song. Make it very clear what types of music you're interested in: country and western all night long; anything and everything salsa; nothing but disco, baby; or a little bit of everything. Confirm that your DJ actually has the songs you've requested and offer to lend him your own CDs if he doesn't. However, while providing your DJ with schedules and song lists and CDs is a good thing, trying to control your music minute by minute is a bad thing. Some people have a certain talent for reading a crowd and picking the tunes to match. This person is your DJ, not you. So let him do his job, playing the music, while you concentrate on yours, dancing to the music all night long.

Tricks DJs Play

DJs, of course, aren't flawless. We've all been to a wedding or two where the DJ just wouldn't stop talking (and talking and talking)— and really, how many times can you play "YMCA" anyway? As it turns out, DJs have their own set of tricks. If your DJ attempts any of the following, start looking for someone else.

PRETEND THEY WON'T TALK Like I said earlier, DJs are not musicians, and fortunately, most of them know this. However, a few of them don't, which is why, I suspect, they wind up doing so much talking: They actually think they're singing. Okay, maybe they don't actually think they're singing, but they do think they're being entertaining. In fact, this is how many DJs bill themselves: as entertainers. If you're not looking for an entertainer, be sure to listen carefully to your DJ's ideas for your reception during your initial meeting, and make sure he listens carefully to yours.

If you realize he never stopped talking about his own ideas, it probably means he never listened to yours and this isn't the DJ for you.

PRETEND TO OWN EVERY SONG Some DJs may claim to own every single album by every single musician in the world. This is pretty unlikely. Look carefully at your DJ's music collection, checking to see that he owns a variety of musical styles and songs you like. You can always loan him copies of the songs you simply can't imagine your wedding without, but a DJ can't be versatile if he doesn't own a versatile selection of music (and by versatile, I don't mean the original, live, and unplugged versions of "YMCA").

PRETEND TO KNOW WHAT THEY'RE DOING Hint: A good DJ doesn't invite everyone out onto the dance floor by hollering, "Couple's skate!"

PRETEND TO HAVE THE PROPER EQUIPMENT DJs are just as guilty as bands at pretending they have all the equipment they need when they really don't. Make sure your DJ is familiar with your reception site (if he's not, have him arrange a visit before your wedding) and confirm that he has everything he thinks he'll need: generators, outlets, microphones, speakers, extension chords, tables, tablecloths. You should also make sure your DJ knows ahead of time where he's actually going to put all of his equipment. Tip: He shouldn't call you the day of the wedding to ask where you think he should set up.

OTHER MUSICAL CONSIDERATIONS

Although the most important thing your musicians, band, and/or DJ should be able to do is play, you will have to consider a few other details: like a contract. Yours should include:

- Date, time, and location of wedding ceremony and/or reception.

- Name of band's manager or other contact person with telephone number (also include a telephone or pager number where the band can be reached the day of the wedding).

- Your and your groom's names and telephone numbers.

- Your site coordinator's or caterer's name and telephone number (emergency number to contact the day of the wedding).

- Name of musicians with acceptable substitutes or size of band/ensemble and types of instruments they're bringing.

- Musicians' arrival time and setup requirements.

- Detailed equipment requirements: stage, power outlets, speakers, etc.

- Other musicians' requirements: dressing rooms, meals, accommodations for overnight performances.

- Musicians' attire.

- Length of performance and specific break information (How many breaks will the musicians take and for how long? Will they play taped music? Will one musician keep performing?).

- Musicians' other responsibilities: acting as emcee, playing specific songs, *not* playing specific songs.

- Detailed information regarding an outdoor event, including band's policy in case of bad weather.

- Total price, including overtime fees, payment schedule, and payment method.

- Refund and cancellation policy.

Other details that may not be included in your contract but that you'll want to discuss with your musicians include: parking information (including where to load and unload equipment), your site's specific musical restrictions, and information regarding the scheduling of your reception. Most bands include a questionnaire with their contract that asks for information that will help them determine the size, style, and appropriate music for your reception. Our band's questionnaire asked for the following information: expected number of guests; age of bride and groom; style of music preferred; whether the wedding party should be introduced and, if so, a complete list of their names; what traditions would be observed throughout the evening: toasts (best man, groom's father, bride's father), cake-cutting, bouquet toss, garter toss, and the most important question of all: the bride and groom's first-dance request. Most bands are willing to play a song unfamiliar to them provided you send them a tape of the song and sheet music far enough in advance (our band was kind enough to learn two songs).

If your ceremony or reception is being held outside, be sure and ask your site's manager if you will need to file for an outdoor music permit. Most communities require you to register an outdoor event with the local police station at least three days before the event and have specific guidelines regarding what types of music may be played and the hours during which the event may take place. Filing for a permit is a fairly simple process, but just one of those things you do not want to forget. Hint: It's much more fun to hit the dance floor at your reception than to be hit with a hefty fine.

Flowers

A ROSE IS A ROSE IS A ROSE

Blue Curiosa roses, Rustique roses, Sahara roses, Esther roses, Magic Silver roses, Oriental Curiosa roses, porcelain roses, rambler roses, coquette roses, tea roses, blush roses, Madam Pompadour roses, miniature roses . . . That's an awful lot of roses. Don't know the difference? Me neither. That's why we hired a florist. That's also why we showed up at our florist's without a clue as to what we were doing. Lucky for us, we had an absolutely fantastic florist who taught us exactly what we needed to know (and delivered some of the most beautiful arrangements I've ever seen). Lucky for you, I'm going to share with you all of the very important lessons we learned about picking out flowers—and a florist—that are right for you.

STOP AND SMELL THE ROSES

Before you set up a single meeting with a single florist, heed the age-old adage to "stop and smell the roses." In other words, before you run willy-nilly to the closest (or most popular) florist to place your order, you really should stop and figure out exactly what it is you'll be ordering. This means a little bit of homework for you and your groom, but I promise it's not hard, and it might even be a little bit of fun. It will also save you and your florist tons of time (which, as you may have noticed, is quickly running out).

Your first assignment is to grab a pen and notebook. Turn to a blank page and copy down the chart I've provided below. This chart looks a lot like the one our florist filled out and should look similar to the one your florist will use. If not, it's still a handy piece of paper to have while discussing with your florist what flowers you'll need for your wedding day.

ITEM	QUANTITY	DESCRIPTION	COST
Bridal bouquet			
Throwaway bouquet (for bouquet toss)			
Bridal crown/wreath			
Individual flowers for hair			
Bridesmaid bouquets			
Flower girl bouquet, basket, or wreath			
Groom boutonniere			
Groomsmen boutonnieres			
Usher boutonnieres			
Father/grandfather boutonnieres			
Ring bearer			
Honor attendant corsages			

ITEM	QUANTITY	DESCRIPTION	COST
Mother/grandmother corsages			
CEREMONY DECORATIONS: altar or canopy, aisle and pew decorations, candles, outdoor and indoor arrangements			
RECEPTION DECORATIONS: Guest tables, buffet tables, bar arrangement, cake tables, bridal table			
MISCELLANEOUS FLOWERS: welcome/thank-you flowers; flowers for bridesmaid luncheon, wedding brunch, or rehearsal dinner			

Now, next to each item, write down the total quantity you'll need for your wedding. Keep in mind all of those plans you and your groom may have for flowers aside from the traditional bouquets and table arrangements: single rosebuds to present to your mother and mother-in-law as you come down the aisle, fresh rose petals for your cake, an assortment of petals for guests to toss while you make your getaway. Each and every one of these flowers—and petals—will have a price. Fortunately, you don't have to fill in that column right now. (Unfortunately, your florist will fill it in for you later.) The column you should fill out right now is the "description" column. Include ideas you might have regarding each item's style, shape, color, and size, as well as notes on types of flowers you like and dislike. Now is also the time to write down any allergies you or your groom may have.

If, however, you haven't the slightest idea what to put here, your next assignment is to find that pile of wedding magazines and books you have stacked next to the couch. Flip through each magazine and book, tearing out or marking pages with pictures of bouquets and arrangements you like. Gardening and lifestyle magazines and books are also good sources for ideas. I even found inspiration in a greeting card or two. Pay attention to the styles and types of flowers that seem appropriate for your wedding, as well as decorations other than flowers that you find particularly striking: candles, mirrors, lanterns, tulle, lace, bows, Chia pets. Your groom may complain a little at first about this exercise. But before long both of you will be chatting rather animatedly about flowers and fragrance and fresh petals and saying completely ridiculous things like, "Look! I really like the way these tulips seem to have arranged themselves!" and "Yes! Their shadows really create interesting patterns on the tablecloth!" If our own experience is any indication, you will even succeed in carrying out such a conversation with absolutely straight faces (not to worry—as soon as the wedding is over, you'll both go back to being completely normal people).

> *Wedding Myth # 26:* **The bridemaids' bouquets have to be the same color as their dresses.** *Dyed-to-match shoes are one thing. Matching bouquets are another thing entirely. Your wedding party's flowers should complement the basic style and color of their attire, not blend in.*

Such an intelligent and stimulating conversation, while perhaps alarming, is an indication that it's time to return to the "description" column. Jot down ideas for specific types of flowers you've decided you're in love with or a general look you have in mind: elaborate topiaries with cascading Madame Pompadour roses; natural, loose arrangements of summer wildflowers; that rather jaunty tulip arrangement you've both become oh so fond of. Also jot down the color of your dress, your bridesmaid's dresses, and your groomsmen's attire. If you can, bring swatches of material or even the actual outfit with you to your florist. This will give her an idea of the style of your wedding as well as ideas for possible color schemes.

By now you should have most of your chart filled out, which means, of course, it's time for another assignment. Turn to a clean piece of paper and make a list of each site you'll need your florist to decorate—ceremony, reception, rehearsal dinner, bridesmaids' luncheon, wedding brunch—as well as the time and date of each event. This way, she'll be able to tell right off the bat whether she's available. She'll also be able to tell what your site looks like without flowers. Some sites, a backyard garden, for example, will need very little decorating. Other sites, a large open loft, may need a lot. Your florist will also need to take her cues from a site's existing decor (if your florist isn't familiar with your site, have her visit it beforehand).

You should also add to your list any major decorative elements or themes you've already picked out. If you're working with your caterer to put together a Caribbean menu, for instance, you'll obviously want your florist to create a certain atmosphere. Think about lush tropical plants and palms—fruits, coconuts, a scattering of sand. And for each woman, a brilliantly colored hibiscus to tuck behind her ear (all the better to limbo with, my dear). To create such elaborate themes, many caterers will work only with certain florists they trust. Many reception sites also have exclusive lists of florists they'll allow to decorate. You might even want to ask your caterer if he'll act as a florist himself.

The final bit of information you'll need to share with your florist, or at least ponder for a while, is how much you plan on spending on all of those flowers—and candles, mirrors, lanterns, tulle, lace, bows, and Chia pets. The list can go on and on, as can the prices for each item. Flowers and decorations are beautiful. They can also be expensive. But since money doesn't grow on trees (your florist knows this better than anybody), take a last look at your chart and put checks by the items that are most important to you and your groom. If you've always envisioned yourselves exchanging vows beneath a beautifully flowering *chuppa,* think about carrying a smaller bridal bouquet. Or, if your heart is set on a brilliantly colored—and sized—bouquet, decorate your *chuppa* with just as beautiful (but less expensive) greenery and ribbons. A good florist will work with all kinds of budgets to create all kinds of weddings. And a *really* good florist will make sure every single one of them is beautiful.

> *Wedding Myth* # 27: **Flowers have to be expensive.** *Cut flowers are expensive because they have to be picked, trimmed, de-thorned, wired, and arranged. Consider buying potted plants and flowers from your local nursery—and then use them after the wedding on your new back porch.*

A ROSE BY ANY OTHER NAME WOULD SMELL AS SWEET

So how do you find your really good florist? Turn in your homework. In other words, go ahead and schedule several appointments with potential florists. They should be pleased and delighted with all of your and your groom's work. They might also be a little confused, as in, "Well, peonies don't actually bloom in the fall, but Japanese anemones are similar and smell just as sweet." They may even offer to show you each and every possible alternative. Hint: Now is not the time to get caught up in the flowers; now's the time to get down to business.

At the first meeting with your florist (or during your first phone conversation), be prepared to ask a lot of questions:

- Is this first consultation free? How many hours of your time can I expect?

- Do you do a lot of weddings? Can I see photographs or sample arrangements you've done?

- Will you be the actual florist who decorates on the day of my wedding? (Larger shops often employ many florists, so make sure you meet with the one who will be decorating your wedding.)

- Will you be decorating any other weddings or events the day of my wedding?

- Are you familiar with my wedding sites? Are there certain arrangements and decorations you would suggest?

- Will you transport ceremony flowers to my reception?

- What flowers will be in season on my wedding day (and therefore less expensive)? If the flowers I want aren't in season, will you be able to get them from another region or country?

- What is your policy regarding substituting flowers? Will you call for my approval?

- If the flowers I want for my bouquet are expensive, can you suggest other types of flowers for the ceremony and reception arrangements to help me stay within my budget? Will you provide a free throwaway bouquet?

- Do you guarantee the flowers you use will be fresh?

- What time will you arrive to set up the flowers? How much time do you need to set up?

- What are your delivery charges?

- Do you provide other types of decorations?

- Do you require a deposit? Is there a payment schedule?

Of course, there are going to be a million more questions that will occur to you as you talk with your potential florist. If your wedding is outside, you may need suggestions for types of flowers that will withstand heat. If your wedding is inside, you may want suggestions for types of flowers that are fragrant (but not too fragrant). The important thing to remember is to ask for what you want. A good florist loves to be creative and prides herself on putting together weddings that are both beautiful and reflective of the couple she's working with. But (trust me on this) she will never think to ask about those Chia pets if you don't.

At a second meeting (or by phone, fax, or e-mail if you're doing the long-distance thing), your florist will present you with a chart of her own. This chart will look a lot like the one you filled out initially but will be complete with exact items, quantities, costs, and complete descriptions of each and every flower she plans on using. She may provide sketches for some of the bouquets and arrangements and should also provide pictures of any specific items you've picked out, such as a gazebo, a fountain, candelabras, etc. Check to make sure the type and style of each item is what you discussed at your first meeting, and be sure and pay close attention to the quantity of each item (a mother of the bride without a corsage is not a happy mother of the bride). Also take a careful look at the total cost (your florist may list separate totals for each event she'll be decorating, so be sure and add these totals together). If the fee is within your budget, great. If not, you may need to ask for some more suggestions on bringing the price down. Your florist may also need to ask you a few more questions about what's really important to you about your wedding.

Wedding Myth # 28: **The bigger the bouquet, the better.** *More flowers aren't prettier, just heavier.*

This may seem like a lot of questions. But remember, your florist needs to make sure she understands your vision for your wedding day, and you need to make sure she's interested in creating that vision. Because, unfortunately, some florists have their own agendas when it comes to decorating. Smitten with their own tastes and talents, they'll ask you few questions and may not even listen to yours. Instead, they will spend a great deal of time saying things like: "Oh, I know exactly what we'll do" and "Don't you worry about it, dear." Hint: You should worry about it, dear, and you shouldn't hire her.

The florist you should hire is the one whose style you like, whose prices are within your budget, and whose talent and personality you trust. Creating flower arrangements is not an exact science. Even when ordering exact flowers, you cannot be certain they will be available. Season conditions vary. Supplies are often limited. Even the quality of available blooms is sometimes unpredictable. And, of course, there are always drought, flood, and other weird weather occurrences that no one can foretell. So, while you may have very specific flowers in mind, you will have to trust your florist to make last-minute decisions regarding the quality and hardiness of your flowers and to make appropriate substitutions. And while you may mean well by checking out the farmer's almanac and calling your florist monthly with weather updates from around the world (after all, if tulips aren't blooming locally in time for your wedding, you can always get them from Hawaii), it really is best to let her handle all of your weather—and other wedding—worries.

THORNY ISSUES

Of course *your* roses won't have real thorns—you're about to pay your florist a lot of money to take those little guys off. But in order to hire a florist, you're going to need to work through a few thorny issues, such as a contract. A basic florist's contract should include the following:

- Your and your groom's name and telephone numbers.

- Your florist's name and telephone numbers (Will she have a cell phone or beeper on the day of the wedding?).

- Date, time, and location of each event (i.e., rehearsal dinner, ceremony, reception).

- Address for delivery if different from the event's location.

- Set up and delivery times for each event.

- A list of each floral arrangement or decoration, including specific types of flowers used, color, quantity, and cost.

- Policy regarding substitutions and guarantee of freshness.

- Delivery charges and overtime fees.

- Amount of deposit and remaining payment schedule (as well as acceptable payment types: cash, check, credit card).

- Cancellation/refund policy.

Be as specific as possible about each point so that there are no surprises—other than beautiful ones—on your wedding day.

You will also need to discuss with your florist any restrictions your ceremony and reception sites may have regarding decorations. Many churches and synagogues restrict the types of decorations you can use, the size of arrangements, the number, and placement. My church, for example, even stipulates that arrangements must be put in the church's own urns (a real problem when we couldn't find them). You should also discuss all of those tricky, logistical issues like: How is she going to get into your wedding site? Will a door be open? Will she need a key? Will she need to return the key to a specific person after the wedding? Is she transporting the ceremony flowers to your reception or to another site? A wonderful way to share your joy with others is to have your florist take leftover arrangements to a local hospital or nursing home. You might also want to discuss ways to preserve your bridal bouquet. Having your flowers dried, pressed, or made into a perfumed potpourri are wonderful ways to remember your flowers long after the wedding's over.

Pictures

TO SHOOT OR NOT TO SHOOT

I'll go ahead and tell you I'm not a big fan of pictures. Okay, not all pictures, just pictures of me. I tend to do this funny thing with my chin. I have a kind of weird smile. And nine times out of ten, my eyes wind up shut. (Even Brian, who claims I am the most beautiful woman in the world, admits that photographs of me are not always spectacular.) Hiring a wedding photographer, then, posed a bit of a dilemma: How, exactly, do you tell a wedding photographer to take pictures of everybody but the bride? This dilemma was soon solved, however, when my sister got her photographs back from her own wedding. Amid the beautiful shots of Shelley and Trevor exchanging vows by the river, my cousin chasing butterflies with his mother's straw hat perched precariously atop his little head, and all of the grandmothers gathered together, faces lined with wrinkles, wisdom, and love, there was not one picture of me (all right, maybe just one, but no more than that).

*Wedding Myth # 29: **Your wedding photographer will automatically know who everyone in your family is.** Not likely. Fax a list of all important family and wedding party members to your photographer a week before the wedding, as well as must-have photographs.*

Later we found out the photographer didn't know I was Shelley's sister, but never mind that, Marisu was hired. She had done a spectacular job of capturing Shelley's wedding, had avoided all of those terribly awkward posed shots I've always hated, and had managed to miss me pretty much completely. Come my wedding day, I was sure I could convince her to miss me again. She was easygoing, low-key; she would understand.

Well, come my wedding day, Marisu was so low-key, for the most part I forgot she was even there. Which is how, I'm guessing, she managed to get all of those stunning pictures. There's the sweet picture: Brian picking me up off the ground in front of the church after the ceremony. The wacky picture: everyone getting down on the dance floor with the band's lead singer. The serious picture: My mother and sister trying to figure out how to fasten all of those buttons on my dress. The seriously painful picture: me trying to keep my head attached as the groomsmen attempt to pull off my veil. And then there's the . . . Okay, okay, you get the point. I love my wedding pictures. My real point, however, is that your wedding pictures should reflect your wedding day. Mine do. Every time I look at them I experience all over again the million emotions I felt that day.

So how do you find your own amazing photographer? First, realize that wedding photographers come in all shapes, sizes, and styles. Your uncle Bob might even try to throw his amateur photographer hat into the ring. The two main types of wedding photographers, however, are traditional wedding photographers, who shoot traditional posed photographs of you and your groom and your families, and photojournalists, who try to capture your wedding spontaneously through mostly candid shots. You might even want to hire a videographer to capture the big day. The following is a discussion of each one's traits, which should give you a better idea of who to hire for your own wedding day.

THE TRADITIONAL WEDDING PHOTOGRAPHER

A traditional wedding photographer is an absolute professional. He or she has been shooting weddings for years and most likely owns his or her own photography studio. He can arrange to take formal studio portraits as well as traditional posed photographs of the actual wedding day. In small and even larger communities, a quality wedding photographer is a well-respected figure and will have worked at most of the ceremony and reception sites in the area. This is convenient, especially if you and your groom are from out of town and are unfamiliar with the area and the sites you've chosen. Many churches and synagogues, as well as some reception sites (historical homes, museums), have restrictions regarding photography, and it will help if your photographer knows these ahead of time. If yours doesn't, make sure to ask your site's coordinator so there are no last-minute surprises. One young bride was surprised to find out the day of her wedding that the church she had picked specifically because of its stained-glass windows didn't allow pictures inside the sanctuary. She wound up with stiff, posed photographs of her and her husband and their families in front of the uninspiring gray stone wall of the church. "Everyone looks beautiful, but a little sad I think." Take the time to research restrictions, as well as other sites in the area that may make the perfect backdrop: a park, your neighbor's rose garden, the Empire State Building.

Unfortunately, in larger cities, setting up a meeting with a traditional wedding photographer is sometimes difficult. Photographers often work for larger studios and many prohibit contact between the bride and groom and the photographer until the actual wedding day, or until a contract is signed. Studios fear you will hire the photographer independently at a lower price, and they will be unable to collect their fee. Many of these studios have wonderful reputations. You may even be familiar with their work, in which case, perhaps it's worth the risk.

Just make sure you meet with your photographer well before the actual time of your wedding to discuss which photographs you'll want taken—or fax a list ahead of time to the studio.

There's also the price of a studio's or photographer's reputation to consider. Traditional wedding photographers' fees can vary widely—from around $500 to as much as $5,000. And generally, the more popular a photographer, the more you can expect to pay for his services. Prices also vary with the size of the package you choose, which includes a specific number of photographs in different sizes (three by five, four by six, five by seven, eight by ten, and eleven by fourteen are the traditional sizes) and a predetermined number of wedding albums. Most traditional wedding photographers keep their negatives (they consider the negatives their property), so choose your package carefully, since having reprints and enlargements made can be expensive. Traditional wedding photographers may provide you with a proof to keep of each photograph. Or, you may be required to choose which proofs to have made into photographs, returning them by a set date. Be sure and ask your photographer for his specific policies.

The most important trait of traditional wedding photographers, however, is the types of pictures they take. In general, traditional wedding photographers take, well, traditional wedding photographs. Hint: They will not take photographs of you and your groom exchanging vows while jumping out of a perfectly good airplane. They will, however, do a perfectly wonderful job of lining up bridesmaids and groomsmen and calming nervous mothers and taking care of unruly ring bearers and making sure everyone is standing straight up with ties and hems straight down, eyes open, flies shut, and big, beautiful smiles on their faces at the count of one-two-three. Traditional wedding photographers will do this exact same thing again and again and again until they are absolutely sure that everyone looks perfect. Another hint: This takes time. Couples hiring a traditional wedding photographer should plan on having all formal photographs taken before the ceremony, since photographers will sometimes require up to three hours for photographs. Traditional wedding photographers are aiming for perfection, and (think of your own ring bearer) perfection takes time.

Wedding Myth # 30: **Wedding photography has to last as long as the reception.** *If you and your groom belong to large families, have formal photographs of you and your families taken before the ceremony and formal photographs of you and your groom taken afterward. Then head to the reception. Otherwise, you'll miss it.*

You can also expect a traditional wedding photographer to take photographs of you and your groom and wedding party in traditional wedding poses. Some of these are rather nice: you and your bouquet, you and your groom holding hands, you and your bridesmaids, your groom and his groomsmen. Some of these, however, may seem rather silly: you staring adoringly at your bouquet, you and your groom looking lovingly at your gleaming wedding bands, your groom and his groomsmen with their thumbs sticking out of their tuxedo pockets at perfect right angles, and you and your bridesmaids throwing your shoes in the air. Be sure and discuss each pose beforehand to save both time and money. There's no sense in wasting a roll of film on silly shots you know you'll never buy.

Also beware of traditional wedding photographers who may act a little silly themselves. Erin's wedding photographer kept squeaking a plastic toy at them to get everybody to smile, "but it really just gave everyone a headache," she says. And Laurie's photographer actually blew a whistle as a cue for everyone to turn around and smile at the camera. "It was one of the only times I've ever been glad my grandmother is hard of hearing."

A traditional wedding photographer will also shoot rather traditional and posed photographs of your reception, making sure to capture such highlights as: you and your groom's entrance as husband and wife, your first dance, the father/daughter dance, the champagne toast, the cutting of the cake, the tossing of the bouquet, the tossing of the garter, the last dance, your exit. You can be sure each significant moment of your wedding will be covered. However, don't be surprised if your photographer directs each and every one of these moments. A best friend of mine recently attended a wedding where the photographer and videographer hovered over the bride and groom the entire evening. "Each time I tried to make my way to the couple, all I could hear was the photographer chastising them, 'Chin up, head this way, no, no, shoulders back, my dear.' It was like they were in a photo shoot. It was ridiculous and completely contrived—plus, I heard from the bride afterward that the videographer smelled like a horse!" If you're worried your photographer may be too obtrusive—especially if you're having a smaller wedding—ask him to shoot from the sidelines.

Traditional wedding photographs can be wonderful mementos of your wedding day for friends and family. By posing in groups, you are assured you will have a photograph of absolutely every bridesmaid, groomsman, and family member. I certainly wouldn't have been missed at my sister's wedding had she hired a traditional wedding photographer. However, the truth is that no matter how silly that "silly shot" or how perfect your chin as you sip your champagne, traditional wedding photographs often fall short of capturing the true, spontaneous emotions of the day: your mom's face as she slips your dress over your head; your face as the flower girl yanks on your veil just to see what will happen; your groom's face as you whisper in his ear that you aren't wearing any underwear. These surprises—these real moments—are often called candid shots. They could also be called nontraditional shots, and if that's what you're looking for, a wedding photojournalist may be the answer.

THE WEDDING PHOTOJOURNALIST

After all of those squeaky plastic toys and shrill silver whistles, a wedding photojournalist can seem like a breath of fresh air. My photographer was a photojournalist, and as I've said, I don't even remember seeing her, much less hearing her. And this is what a photojournalist is all about. Instead of trying to direct or create each and every moment of your wedding, a photojournalist will quietly and unobtrusively capture your wedding as each moment unfolds. Like a journalist, she is telling a story—in all of its spontaneity, gaiety, even sobriety. Weddings, after all, are full of all sorts of emotions and expressions—not just those big, beautiful smiles. One of my favorite photographs from our wedding, for instance, is an intense group huddle of me, my sister, and Brian as we ponder what to do about the volume of the band (it was really, really loud). We are not grinning goofily at the camera, but rather looking seriously at one another. The photograph is a perfect candid shot of a very real moment.

In order to capture these candid shots, photojournalists aren't exactly silly, but can be rather sneaky. I've heard of photographers climbing up trees, hiding in shrubs, and I'm not sure where Marisu was when she shot the photograph of all of our groomsmen's butts, but I can bet you they were entirely unaware of her presence. A good photojournalist will go to creative lengths to get these fun, candid shots. But "fun" and "candid" do not mean "amateur." Although spontaneous moments may look easy to catch on film, they're not. Look carefully at your photographer's sample albums for overly blurry shots or for photographs where someone consistently has his or her head cut off. And be absolutely sure and check references.

While photojournalists will pay close attention to capturing the perfect emotions of your wedding day, they may not pay close attention to capturing the perfect poses (they're waiting for you to strike a pose, remember?). That can mean a variety of things: a crooked tie, a crooked veil, perhaps even one of those unsightly double chins (tip: keep your chin up!). In photographs of Brian and his groomsmen, for instance, Brian has his arms thrown around his friends in almost every shot. While I'm certain this was a spontaneous motion, the result in the pictures is that his buttoned jacket is all bunched up and his tie sticks out awkwardly. He was also the victim of the bridesmaids' enthusiastic use of deodorant. Dressed in sleeveless dresses—and particularly prone to hugging—they left telltale stripes of deodorant on his navy jacket. And photojournalists who do not shoot posed shots at all may miss an important family or wedding party member completely. Provide your photographer with a list of important shots, or have a friend point out important guests.

The prices of wedding photojournalists also vary. In general, they charge either by the day, or hour, and per roll of film they shoot. Their fees tend to be lower than a traditional wedding photographer's but do not include the cost of wedding albums or reprints from the negatives. Most photojournalists will return the negatives to you to develop on your own, as well as a proof of each photograph. This is often cheaper than having a traditional wedding photographer put together your album for you and is certainly convenient for ordering reprints and enlargements (make sure your photographer numbers each proof and negative for easy ordering). However, before you hit the corner one-hour photo shop, ask your photographer for a recommendation of a good printer. Local newspaper and magazines may also be able to direct you to quality photography labs.

Traditional wedding photographers will do a super job of taking perfect photographs of the people at your wedding (what they look like, what they're wearing). Photojournalists will do a super job of capturing these people's personalities (who they are, what they're doing). A good photojournalist will also capture perfectly the personality of you and your groom, paying close attention to all of the details that make your wedding special. And, after all, you've just spent a lot of time personalizing your wedding; shouldn't your wedding photographs be personal, too?

Wedding Myth # 31: ***You have to have a wedding video.*** *If you don't want a wedding video, no one, including your mother, his mother, or his film-school brother, should talk you into having one.*

THE WEDDING VIDEOGRAPHER

Brides pretty much everywhere are of two minds on the whole wedding video issue: "Yes! Yes! We absolutely must have a wedding video!" Or "No way! We are absolutely not having a wedding video!" I understand both points of view. On the one hand, a video can be a wonderful memento from a day that goes by way (way) too quickly. It's also a wonderful way to catch a lot of the action you're going to miss as the bride and groom. Laura's biggest surprise was watching her eighty-year-old granddad cut a rug with all of her bridesmaids: "I have never in my life seen him move like that—every time we watch the video it makes me laugh." And, since you'll be the last one coming down the aisle, a video may be your only chance to actually see your ceremony: the flower girl slyly dumping her basket of petals in a pile before sashaying off to her mother. The ring bearer scooping up the petals and carrying them to the minister. And, even more special, your grandmother's face lighting up as your dad walks you toward the altar.

Videos can also be wonderful presents for family and friends who can't be with you on your wedding day. Most of Sarah's family, for instance, was from France. Her groom's family was from Portugal. "It was sad that so many people couldn't be with us on our wedding day, but the wedding video was a great way to include them. My great-grandmother was able to see the veil she had sent over for me to wear. And the videographer interviewed our guests saying hello to everyone who couldn't be there."

Videos also make special family heirlooms. Kimmy and Davis had their wedding video professionally edited and included photographs of the both of them growing up. They also had their videographer include all of their favorite Sinatra songs. Seven years and two kids later, and amid all of the Disney videos on their shelves, their wedding video is still one of their four-year-old daughter's favorites: "At family gatherings, the video inevitably comes out and she dances around and around. When we had the video made, we knew our wedding was a day we wanted to share with our parents—we didn't realize that it would also be a wonderful day to share with our children."

On the other hand, a video can often feel intrusive. Everyone has a bad memory of a particularly zealous videographer sticking a microphone in their face. Betsy says, "I always felt so awkward at those moments and I certainly didn't want to feel that way on my wedding day. I didn't want to feel like I was performing." And many brides just feel videos are unnecessary. "Our photographs are beautiful and I'll always treasure the story they tell," Ann says, "but I didn't want to have to watch a video and be, like, 'Oh no, I'm walking too fast, or too slow' or thinking, 'What in the world is my hair doing?' My memory of my wedding day is enough—it's perfect and I can play it over and over."

Videos as well as photographs may also be restricted, or even prohibited, in your church or synagogue to preserve the sanctity of the ceremony. Our church, for example, restricts cameras and videos to the balcony in the back of the church. I've seen videos from other weddings in the church and all you can see are the backs of the guests—and the actual bride and groom are tiny. Even with close-up shots, a video didn't seem worth it. Plus, a videographer's services can also be quite expensive, a professionally edited video costing up to $2,000. However, videographers, like photographers, come in all shapes, sizes, and styles, and if you really want a video of your wedding day, you should be able to find a videographer who matches both your personality and your pocketbook.

Before hiring your videographer, be sure and check out their equipment, their references, and, more important, their videos, paying close attention to the quality of the picture, the quality of the sound, and, of course, the videographer's style. Stay away from videographers who always seem to be in people's faces—or who always seem to be at the bar. Liz recalls her wedding day: "Halfway through our reception we realized we hadn't seen our videographer in a while so I sent Mike to find him. It turns out he was at the bar and was so drunk he could hardly stand. We told him to leave but kept his video camera, and my parents returned it the next week. We got our deposit back and actually had more fun shooting the video ourselves. But really, check for references."

BEFORE PHOTOS

Before the photographer and/or videographer you hire takes a single shot, you'll need to first draw up a contract. This very important piece of paper should include the following:

- The photographer's/videographer's name (if you are using a studio, the contract should still list the name of the actual person who will be shooting your wedding), as well as telephone, cell, and pager numbers.

- Your name and telephone numbers.

- The location and address of ceremony and reception sites.

- The time of the wedding.

- The number of hours and/or days your photographer/videographer will shoot.

- The total number of rolls of film your photographer will shoot, including an estimated number of images per roll, cost per roll, and type: black-and-white and/or color.

- The final length of your edited video.

- Specifics regarding special effects and editing techniques.

- The details of your package, including the specific number of photographs, their sizes, and the number of completed albums.

- Delivery date of your proofs, negatives (if your photographer returns them to you), finished albums, and videos.

- Policy regarding negatives (even if your photographer keeps the negatives, you may have the option to buy them after a certain period of time).

- Total number of cameras and/or assistants your photographer/videographer will be using.

- Total cost, including overtime fees and payment schedule.

- Cancellation/refund policy.

You will also want to discuss with your photographer/videographer the actual logistics of your wedding day. Will you be taking photographs before or after your ceremony? If you and your groom don't want to see each other until that very special moment when you first walk down the aisle, arrange for your photographer to shoot pictures of you and your family and bridesmaids, and then pictures of your groom with his family and groomsmen before the ceremony. Afterward, she can pull you and your groom aside quickly for photographs—when both of you will be absolutely glowing and those smiles will be anything but posed.

Talk about shooting photographs outside and inside, and discuss what percentage of your photographs you would like to be posed versus candid. You will also want to decide whether color or black-and-white film is more appropriate for your wedding. Color photographs will obviously capture all the color of the day—the linens and ribbons you worked so hard to coordinate, the brilliant colors in your bouquet, and the amazing shades of the sky as the clouds finally clear and the sun breaks through. Black-and-white photographs, on the other hand, tend to capture the emotions of the day. Faces are more pronounced and expressive and photographs feel romantic and timeless. Of course, why not have the best of both worlds and have your photographer take some of both?

You will also want to decide whether to have a formal bridal portrait made. These portraits are made of the bride in her bridal gown and veil a couple of months before the wedding and are often displayed at the reception. Portraits can be either photographed or painted by a portrait artist. Some couples also choose to have an engagement portrait taken in formal or casual attire to submit along with their engagement and/or wedding announcement. Having an engagement portrait taken is also a good way to meet your photographer and get to know each other's personalities. Some couples even display their portraits at the reception as well. Jennifer and Dana, for instance, had their portrait—taken of the two of them and their two golden retrievers—framed with a wide matte border around the picture. At the reception, guests used gold pens to sign the matte border with best wishes for a happy marriage. It's a beautiful picture and a wonderful keepsake from their wedding day. Dana also admits it was a good way to "sneak in the dogs."

HOW TO FIRE THE PHOTOGRAPHER

Unfortunately, not all of your vendors will do a perfect job. Liz's drunk videographer certainly didn't, and it was perfectly appropriate to ask him to leave the reception. Nancy's photographer didn't do a perfect job either: Her grandmother's dress was hiked halfway up her leg in dozens of photos, and although the photographer had promised she would digitally copy flames onto the candles that had burnt out during the ceremony, she didn't. Unfortunately, Nancy didn't discover this until after the actual wedding day. So what did she do? She complained.

"The frustrating thing about wedding photographs is that you have a one-time shot at getting them right. You are never going to get all the people back together again in the same outfits for a retake. So people should think about the different poses and shots they want and not be bashful about letting the photographer know. Unfortunately, there wasn't anything we could do about our photos. But there was something we could do about the photographer. We reported her to the studio, and after they realized what a poor job she did, they fired her."

Not everything is going to go perfectly at your wedding. After all, accidents do happen. But your vendors should do the job you've hired them for, and if they don't, you should always complain. Make an official complaint to the company you've hired them from or to the Better Business Bureau, who will record your complaint and warn potential customers who inquire about the vendor's history. Being a bride is hard enough without having to worry about drunk, smelly, or just lousy photographers. So, do all of those other brides out there a favor and have her fired.

Invitations

THE NAME GAME

Brides and grooms should be prepared to mail out their wedding invitations four to eight weeks before the actual wedding. They should be prepared to order their invitations three months before the wedding. And they should be prepared to start putting together their guest list and picking out their invitations six months before the wedding. How do I know this? Because Brian and I didn't abide by any of these rules and mailing our wedding invitations turned into what I can only call a complete catastrophe. This was bad for us, of course, but turns out to be rather good for you: You get to learn from our mistakes. I've put together the following guidelines based on these mistakes, guaranteeing that ordering, addressing, and mailing your invitations takes place smoothly, simply, and, most important, on time.

CREATING A GUEST LIST

The very first step in ordering your invitations is to create a guest list. Way back in the budget chapter, you should have collected preliminary lists from your families and even created one of your own. Now is the time to finalize these lists and to gather an address for each guest. You may choose to create your list on a computer. Many software companies as well as wedding web sites have programs for creating and keeping track of guest lists. However, if you don't have access to a computer or are looking for something more portable, a simple solution is to create a file-card box, placing each guest's name and address on an index card and filing it alphabetically. As responses come in, you can mark on each card whether or not the guest plans on attending and make notes about arrival times, dietary restrictions, or baby-sitter needs. This is also a great way to keep track of gifts as they arrive. Simply find the guest's card and record their gift—as well as the date you sent out their thank-you.

As you record your guests' names, be sure and find out their full names, as well as the names of their children if you're including the little ones in the big day. Depending on the formality of your wedding, you may also be required to use a guest's first and middle names, as well as their titles (Dr., Jr., Maj. Gen.). Gathering all of this information will, of course, take time, so enlist your families' and friends' help. Your mother can take charge of gathering the addresses for her guest list. Your groom's mother can take charge of her guest list. And if you have a friend who was married recently, ask her for the addresses of all of your mutual friends.

Wedding Myth # 32: **You have to invite everyone you know to your wedding.** This is absolutely not true. You can always elope.

CHOOSING A STATIONER

After you've completed your guest list, the next step is to choose a stationer. Ask your friends (especially recent brides) and family for recommendations and visit stationery stores in you area. Mail-order stationers as well as Internet stationers also offer quality invitations and can be less expensive alternatives to some of the high-end national stationery companies. Brian and I used a small engraving company in North Carolina and paid well below half of what we would have paid a Manhattan stationer. You may also choose to buy invitation computer software and create your own wedding invitations.

While considering which stationer to use, look closely at the company's sample invitations as well as the services they offer. Do they offer a variety of styles and types of paper (standard cotton paper as well as Japanese rice paper or vellum)? Can they use color ink? Will they include a family crest or other special design element? Can they design or print maps and directions? Will they fold, tissue, and insert invitations into inner envelopes for you? Do they offer calligraphy services? Will they print other items like beverage napkins or matchbooks? Do they sell thank-you notes as well as monogrammed cards? You can expect many companies to offer discounts if you order all of your wedding materials through them. As you begin the ordering process, you can also expect to have what can seem like a million questions. A good stationer will be accessible and help you work out the answers to all of your questions, helping you create the perfect wedding invitation (custom-making one if necessary) and making sure all of your materials get to you on time.

CHOOSING AN INVITATION

Once you have decided on a stationer, it's time to choose an invitation. This means looking even more closely at the stationer's samples, choosing paper, ink color, border designs, trim, illustrations, size, font style, and type of printing. As you consider your choices, keep in mind the formality of your wedding. For formal weddings, most brides and grooms choose traditional invitations made from heavy white or ivory paper with black engraving. Even this classic choice, however, comes in a variety of options: paper containing cotton versus acid-free paper without cotton, for instance. Each option, of course, comes with its own price, so consider whether you think your guests will even notice if your invitations contain cotton before deciding to pay the extra money. Also consider that the heavier card stock (and the more lace, trim, and ribbons) you choose, the more postage the invitation will require.

Choosing a print type can also affect the price of your invitations. Engraving is still the traditional choice and is used on most formal invitations. The process produces the clean-cut, elegant letters for which genuine engraving is known, with print slightly raised on the front of the invitation and slightly "bruised," or indented, on the back. Engraving is time-consuming, with much of the work done by hand, and is the most expensive form of printing. A less expensive option is a process called thermography, in which letters are raised on the front but are flat on the back. If you're having a small wedding, you may even consider handwriting your invitations. Etiquette books say this is perfectly acceptable, and it's a personal way of inviting your friends to share in your special day.

For less formal weddings, or even for formal weddings where the bride and groom don't feel tied to tradition, creating an unusual and personalized wedding invitation can be a fun way to express your and your groom's personalities and convey to all of your guests the style of your wedding. Heidi and James, for instance, both avid hikers, were having a small outdoor wedding on top of one of their favorite mountains. They wanted their invitations to capture both the intimacy of the occasion and the beauty of the site. They asked an artist friend for help and she designed a long, narrow invitation with a pattern of leaves cascading across it. As a special surprise, she even had T-shirts made with the same design for each of the wedding guests.

CHOOSING ENCLOSURES

While choosing your invitations, you'll also need to decide on which enclosures to include. Many brides and grooms choose to enclose reception cards, a small card separate from your wedding invitation, inviting guests to the reception after the ceremony. Many more brides and grooms, however, choose to combine the ceremony and reception information on one invitation. Not only is this proper, it's also less expensive.

You should also consider whether or not to include response cards. Some etiquette books frown on the practice, advising brides and grooms to simply have the letters "RSVP" engraved in the bottom-left corner of their invitations. Guests then write their own responses, either accepting the invitation with pleasure or regretfully declining. However, I can think of only a handful of our guests who would actually have written such responses. That's why response cards were invented. Response cards come in different designs. Some resemble small forms, with lines to fill out and boxes to check. We chose a simpler style, a blank card, which read, "The favour of a reply is requested by the twenty-second of May" (response cards should be returned two weeks before your wedding). Guests were able to tell us whether they were able to attend, offer us personal notes of congratulations, and some were even inspired to doodle a picture or two. They were a fun, and funny, way to find out who was coming to the wedding and, even now, they make great keepsakes.

> *Wedding Myth #33: **Family and friends invited from out of town will not come.** This is their excuse to finally have that family reunion they've always talked about. This is their chance to finally take a much-needed vacation. They'll come.*

If many of your guests will be coming from out of town, you may want to include a separate enclosure with directions and hotel and flight information. Many stationers will print maps and directions on the same paper stock as your wedding invitations if you provide them with the information. Or, feel free to create these enclosures on your own. I picked out an elegant bond paper in the same color as the invitations and printed directions from the Atlanta, Georgia, airport to Athens, Georgia, as well as information regarding hotels in the area.

Some brides and grooms may choose to send this information out separately, but do make sure to send it. Brian and I accidentally left this information out of some of our guests' invitations, and our phone rang off the hook for weeks. If you're certain most of your guests have access to a computer, consider e-mailing the information. Of course, just because you include directions in your guests' invitations doesn't mean your guests will actually keep these directions handy.

To ensure most people actually show up at your wedding, include directions in your guest's hotel rooms along with a welcome letter, a schedule of events, a guide to the area, any special restaurant or entertainment recommendations, and perhaps even a fruit basket or gift of some kind. One bride I've heard of even went so far as to tape a set of directions to each of her friends' and family members' cars' sun visors. A great idea—just remember to tell everyone you put them there.

Finally, if you are having a large wedding and are worried about seating all of your guests, you might also want to send out "within the ribbon" cards to people who are to be seated in the pews just behind the bride's and groom's mothers. This ensures that close friends and family (no matter how late they're running) will be sitting close enough to see and hear you and your groom throughout the ceremony.

WORDING INVITATIONS

Once you've chosen your invitations and enclosures, it's time to start the writing process. This means finalizing the date, time, and day of your wedding, learning the correct spelling of your reception and ceremony sites, as well as their addresses, deciding on whose names should be included on the invitation, and choosing the proper wording and order.

All of this will seem very complicated (especially when parents are divorced and absolutely everybody wants to be included on the invitation) until you realize that your stationer has been figuring out these kinds of problems for years and will help answer all of your questions.

To make this process even easier, your stationer will have dozens of sample invitations on hand so you can find the style, as well as the wording, that most closely matches your own wedding situation.

The most important thing for you to keep in mind is that the more formal your wedding is going to be, the more formal your invitation should be. No initials or nicknames should be used for either yours, your groom's, or your parents' names. All words and numbers (including times and addresses) should be spelled out. And if your ceremony is being held in a place of worship, the request line should read "request the honour of your presence." If the ceremony is being held outside a house of worship (a park, club, or hotel, for instance), the line should read "request the pleasure of your company." And when in doubt, ask. Your stationer, your mother, a best friend all will help you make sure your invitation is perfectly beautiful *and* perfectly proper.

ORDERING INVITATIONS

Once you've picked your stationer, chosen your invitations and enclosures, and worded your invitations as carefully as possible, it's time to place your order. As I mentioned earlier, this should be done approximately three months before your wedding date—earlier if possible. If there are any errors (yours or your stationer's) in your final invitations, it may take awhile to have them reprinted. If you are addressing your own invitations, be prepared to make a few errors here as well. Calligraphy pens are often more difficult to use than brides imagine, and many an ink-smeared invitation has wound up in the trash can. You should also be prepared for your guest list to grow. Stationers recommend ordering an extra twenty-five invitations to take care of such surprises, as well as ordering an extra fifty to a hundred outer envelopes to take care of those smeared envelopes and any spelling errors you are bound to make. Ordering extra invitations and envelopes is far less expensive and time-consuming than having them reprinted. Stationers also recommend having your outer envelopes shipped early, so you can begin addressing them as soon as possible.

Wedding Myth # 34: **No one in your family needs to see the wedding invitation before you place your order.** *If you make a mistake (misspelling his mother's name, leaving his family off the invitation entirely), you may not end up married after all.*

When placing your order, be sure and get a delivery schedule from your stationer. Depending on what type of printing you choose (engraving, thermography), most companies will ship your order in a month to a month and a half (envelopes can be shipped in one to two weeks). If you're running behind schedule yourself, rush delivery is generally available for an extra charge. You should also ask to proof your invitation before it is actually printed. And, you should have in writing your company's policy if an error is made. If the error is made by the stationer, they should reprint the invitations at no cost to you. If the error is the result of your mistake, many companies will agree to redo the order and will charge you only the production costs.

ADDRESSING INVITATIONS

Once your invitations are ready—and once you've had a chance to ooh and aah over them—it's time to start addressing them. This step, incidentally, is where Brian and I made our first blunder, so I'm offering this advice: If you are sending out more than 100 invitations, hire someone to address them for you. Many stationers offer both printing and calligraphy services. Or ask a friend with nice handwriting to address them as her gift to you. I would gladly have paid someone to address our wedding invitations, but there was the little problem of an unfinished guest list. In fact, at the time Brian and I placed our invitation order, our guest list consisted of a green folder filled with five marked-up pages of typed addresses, Post-it Notes with barely legible names and numbers, and envelopes with return addresses from guests we had recently received letters from.

Hence, we were on our own. Or, more accurately, *I* was on my own. Brian has completely illegible handwriting, and although he was more than willing to help, I was unwilling to let him. Fortunately, his mother has absolutely beautiful handwriting and, sensing I was on the verge of a nervous breakdown, invited us out for the weekend to help with the invitations. So, while Brian and his stepfather discussed the merits of bad penmanship, his mother and I addressed all 600 outer and inner envelopes. The outer envelopes should include the full names of your guests and their addresses—no abbreviations. Inner envelopes may include either the guest's title and last name (Ms. Clark), or if your wedding is less formal, simply the guest's first name (Aunt Beverly). We completed this task relatively painlessly, making just a few mistakes, which brings me to my next piece of advice: If you're addressing your own invitations, invite a mother, sister, or friend to help. The process will go by much more quickly—and you'll have a lot more fun.

BUYING STAMPS

Once you've addressed your invitations, buying stamps is going to seem like a breeze. I said *seem*. There wasn't anything breezy at all about my four encounters with the post office. Why four? Once to have the invitation weighed. Twice to have the invitation reweighed with the enclosure for out-of-town guests that I had forgotten to bring along on the first trip. And since I had neglected to count how many invitations needed the enclosures and how many didn't (which meant some invitations needed 33-cent stamps and some 55-cent stamps), I had to return a third time. On the third trip, however, the post office was out of 33-cent heart stamps, so I returned a fourth and final time to have all the invitations stamped and finally (finally) mailed. How to avoid four trips to the post office: Weigh your invitations with all enclosures, no matter how small an enclosure seems. And, if some invitations will contain different enclosures from others, have these invitations weighed separately. Above all, know ahead of time how many of each stamp you'll need. Simply flip through your file box, counting the total number of out-of-town guests and in-town guests, perhaps even marking each guest's card with a different color sticker (blue for in town; red for out of town). This will also help you when you're reserving blocks of hotel rooms for out-of-town guests and when you're figuring out your rehearsal-dinner guest list. Fortunately, once you've mastered the art of sending out wedding invitations, sending out rehearsal-dinner invitations really is a breeze.

ASSEMBLING INVITATIONS

Once you've successfully purchased your stamps, it's time to assemble your invitations. I am not going to bore you with how long it took me to figure this out (my brain was still a little frazzled from the stamp episode). I'll simply tell you how it should be done. If your invitations need to be folded, fold the invitation with the lettering on the outside, facing up. Place the tissue on top (optional). If you are including reception cards, place the reception card faceup on the tissue with its lettering parallel to that of the invitation. Slide the response card under the flap of the response envelope (do not put the card inside the envelope) with the lettering facing forward so you can read it. Place the response card and envelope on top of the reception card. The invitation and all enclosures (reception cards, response cards, maps) are then inserted into the inner envelope with the fold of the invitation at the bottom of the envelope. Last, place the inner envelope (do not seal it) in the outer envelope with the guest's name facing the back, so the guest can read her name when she opens the invitation.

LICKING ENVELOPES

With all of the invitations assembled, it was time to seal them. I had invited my friend Lizzie over to help with this process and I'll go ahead and tell you we did not relish licking 300 envelopes. Envelope glue doesn't taste very good and, well, there are a dozen or so urban legends floating around based on people who have died while licking wedding invitations.

So how *should* you seal your envelopes? Water and paper towels will work if you're really, really neat (Lizzie and I weren't really, really neat and ruined well over a dozen invitations). A small wet sponge works even better. But your best bet is to head to your local stationer. Most stores sell a variety of tools for sealing envelopes that are easy—and safe—to use.

There are many, many thoughts and details that go into the process of ordering, addressing, assembling, and mailing wedding invitations. You cannot be quite sure what they are going to be until you do it yourself. You may decide to send out traditional engraved invitations. You might decide to hand-write and illustrate a warm invitation to only your closest friends. Who knows, you may even decide to send out a group e-mail. But whatever you decide, it will take time. Time to think about and time to execute. Even if you decide to hire someone to execute the process for you, you'll need to make sure they have enough time to complete the task. Wedding invitations don't have to go into the mail until four to eight weeks before the wedding, but as Brian and I learned, there is much to do between now and then. So, take our advice (and Lizzie's, too) and start now.

The Dress

FROM SAMPLE SALE TO SEAMSTRESS

Ta-dah! Here comes the bride and, most important, the wedding dress. Some girls start dreaming of this wonderful white creation at a very early age. My cousin, for instance, was somewhere around five years old when she started prancing regularly around the house with a white slip over her head and describing in detail the "bee-yoo-ti-ful" white dress she would wear one day. I, however, have to admit to being a little daunted by the prospect of putting on such a "bee-yoo-ti-ful" white dress, and when I eventually did, it happened completely by accident.

I was shopping with a friend, intent on adding a few items to my spring wardrobe, when we found ourselves in a boutique that just happened to have a wedding dress hanging in the back. Convinced it was time I tried on just such a dress, Jessica pushed me into a dressing room. One look in the dressing room mirror, however, and I was convinced I wasn't. Leaving the white lace dress dancing crookedly on the hanger, I immediately dragged Jessica into another shop where I paraded around in a beautiful, long, silk, sleeveless, red dress. This, I thought, as I saw my reflection, was *me*.

And then, it hit me: While I wasn't exactly prepared to walk down the aisle in a red dress (nor were many people, Brian included, prepared to let me), I knew I needed to find a dress that made me feel the same way the red one did. I wanted to feel beautiful but not sexy. Elegant but not formal. Simple but not plain. Fun but not silly or frilly or bouncy or flouncy or lacy or crazy. (Sound like a tall order? Consider the model bride-to-be who requested that a famous designer make her a wedding dress that made her feel—but not necessarily look—naked.) The point is, your wedding dress should reflect your personality as well as the mood, feelings, and visions you have of your wedding day.

Finding a wedding dress, then, is like finding yourself, which is why when your best friends tell you *you'll just know*, they're actually right. You may have a hard time believing this, but recognizing yourself when you see her is generally pretty easy. You put on a dress and say something along the lines of, "Ah, yes, that's me," and then you might do something silly like laugh and giggle or even cry. Finding yourself can be emotional. Some of my best friends told me finding a wedding dress was a bit like falling in love. I think it's a bit like falling in love with yourself. You should feel every bit as beautiful, confident, and special as you are. And guess what that makes you? Yep—a bride.

So where in the world do you begin to look for yourself? My own journey took me to a sample sale, a consignment shop, and, finally, to a seamstress. I'll also share with you some of the other places brides-to-be have found themselves. But remember: There are a gazillion dresses out there; there's only one of you, so the hunt may take some time. It may also take no time at all. But you will find yourself. You will find a wedding dress that says *me*, even if it happens completely by accident.

DESIGNER BOUTIQUES AND TRUNK SHOWS

In big cities, there are dozens of wedding designers with their own private boutiques. An appointment is required solely so they can lavish you with individual attention. In fact, the whole experience is lavish. Service is lavish. Dressing rooms are lavish. Dresses are lavish. Prices are lavish. Don't be fooled by these newer boutiques with wispy slips of white dresses showcased in a kind of chic minimalism. They have lavish prices, too.

However, even if you can't afford a designer dress, you may want to visit a boutique anyway. Lavish is often fun. I mean, weddings are all about dreams, right? Plus, it's a great way to figure out which styles and designs you like that a seamstress may be able to re-create for less. One bride-to-be actually took her seamstress with her to a boutique so she could study how the dress was made. Other brides-to-be recommend taking pictures if the boutique or store will allow it. Friends and family who may not be able to sneak away at lunchtime with you can compare photos and help you choose the perfect dress.

Many designers also have trunk shows in major metropolitan cities where they showcase their latest designs. You may be able to order directly from the designer or from the store where the show is being held. Other wedding vendors, including florists, photographers, and cake designers, are often present at trunk shows and are available to talk with brides-to-be.

BRIDAL SALONS AND DEPARTMENT STORES

For brides-to-be who don't have enough time to visit individual boutiques, wedding salons and department stores carry a variety of different designers' dresses. Both are wonderful places to try on a range of styles in a wide range of prices. Both also generally carry bridesmaid dresses, so invite all of your bridesmaids along to try on dresses at the same time you do. If you are looking for a simple wedding dress, you may even consider looking at a bridesmaid dress yourself in white or ivory. Lisa, for example, was having a very simple ceremony on a Wednesday at city hall. Although she knew some couples show up in blue jeans, she wanted the occasion to feel a little more special. On a trip to have a bridesmaid dress altered for her friend's wedding, she actually found the same dress in off-white, which just happened to be on sale for $50. Wedding boutiques and department stores also generally carry veils, gloves, shoes, and other wedding accessories. Or you may be able to order them from a catalog. Many boutiques and department stores require an appointment, so make sure you call ahead.

Wedding Myth # 35: **Wedding shoes have to be uncomfortable.** *No, they don't. And if they are, take them off, put them back in the box, and return them after the wedding. Tip: Paint your toenails just in case.*

SAMPLE SALE

A very basic definition of a sample sale might go something like this: "an occasion where designers put their wares on sale in odd places like hotels and apartment suites." But as with most things to do with weddings, there is a lot more to a sample sale than meets the eye. Just ask Pat, a very nice, very obliging young friend of mine who sometimes speaks before he thinks. Such was the case when he agreed to attend a Vera Wang sample sale with me.

The sample sale started at 9 A.M. on Saturday morning at the Pennsylvania Hotel. We arrived at around 8:45 A.M., took the elevator to the eighteenth floor, stepped off, and gaped. The entire universe had arrived ahead of us. In a line that was at least a mile long was a stream of women—women from New York, women from New Jersey, women from Pennsylvania, women from Idaho, women from (I'm sure I saw a few) other planets. Some had high hair; some had low hair; some had no hair. And most had diamonds. Those who didn't were there to help their friends who did. They all also had come with magazines in hand, newspapers in tow, breakfast and lunch preprepared and tucked neatly beneath their arms. I was nervous. Pat was scared.

I wasn't even sure where the sample sale was until a woman ahead of us in line told me (a little too smugly, I thought) that it was in two rooms after the room we could see. The line snaked through two hallways, around each of the two rooms, until you were in the homestretch to *the room*. Five hours later, we made it into *the room*. Ten minutes later, we were back on the street.

I had found nothing. Tried on nothing. Bought nothing. What I *had* done was wander through racks of tulle, mounds of netting, and a sea of big, bouncy things that in no way resembled the simple sheath I was searching for. What Pat had done was follow me through the racks of tulle, mounds of netting, and a sea of bouncing, half-naked women (one of whom threw a green satin heel at him), praying earnestly that I would hurry up and find the simple sheath I was looking for. He never had the chance to give me any dress advice, but he did find the opportunity to be completely honest: "You owe me." So I bought him lunch—BBQ, french fries, and onion rings—and we laughed. What else can you do?

Tips: Arrive early or arrive late. Show up at 5 A.M. and be in and out by 9:30 A.M. If you do the math, you've waited for four hours, but you get first pick of all the beautiful, perfect dresses you know are just waiting for you. Or arrive late, around 3:30 or 4 P.M. Most people have given up by this point and have gone home. You'll be in and out in about forty-five minutes, and the salespeople swear they keep bringing out more dresses throughout the day. Also important: Bring a full-length mirror. They don't provide mirrors or even dressing rooms, so be prepared to throw modesty to the wind and drop your drawers just about anywhere. The prize is a half-price Vera Wang dress, so what's a little modesty more or less? And before you pick a friend to go along with you, make sure he or she has a good sense of humor. It's going to be a long day.

CONSIGNMENT SHOP

After the sample sale fiasco, I tried a newly opened wedding dress consignment shop, which sold both used bridal wear and unused designer samples. This time, I took Jessica and Robin along on the trip, and although I didn't find a dress I was interested in here either, I tried absolutely every dress on.

Consignment shops can be a treasure trove of amazing dresses at prices well below retail. Ask when new donations typically come in and make appointments at regular intervals. Most consignment stores will alter dresses for you at an additional cost, or will recommend someone who can. Ask for the store's honest opinion regarding any stains that may appear on a dress. Some can be cleaned, but some, unfortunately, cannot. Consignment stores will also generally hold a dress for you for a small deposit so you can bring your mother or best friend back for their opinion. You might also decide to donate your own dress after your big day.

BRIDAL BUILDING

My search for a wedding dress continued a month or so later at New York's bridal building, a wonderful option for brides who live in the area or are willing to travel to find a good deal. Home to many designers' showrooms, the bridal building opens its doors to brides-to-be every Saturday. Designers, attempting to sell off last season's designs, offer sample and new dresses to the public at up to a 50 percent discount. The result, of course, is a bit like a Vera Wang sample sale. Brides arrive from all over with friends, mothers, sisters, cousins (one even came with her groom-to-be) to sort through sample after sample after sample, which may or may not be hanging neatly on racks. Many showrooms also sell bridesmaid dresses, which is a great idea if you can round up all of your bridesmaids on a Saturday (or at least know their sizes). Modesty was again thrown to the wind, with many brides-to-be trying on dresses wherever they found them.

Jessica and I joined the fray, sorting through sizes and styles, tripping over trims, trains, and each other, and even occasionally trying on a dress or two, until I became completely depressed. I was tired of trying on dresses. I was tired of looking at dresses. I was tired of looking at people looking at dresses. I needed a dress. I wanted a dress. But I didn't want to have to make another appointment or waste another Saturday to find one. I was just about to give up all hope and head to the nearest diner when Jessica pushed me into the last and final showroom.

SEAMSTRESS

And here is where I found the perfect solution to my wedding dress madness: a designer and seamstress named Shoshana. For hours, she calmly helped me try on various wedding dresses until I found a skirt and a material I liked. Then she spent another hour with me as I tried on various wedding dress tops she had made so I could mix and match. "Just like Colorforms!" Jessica pointed out, which is why I probably felt so at ease. It was fantasy, it was fun, and, finally, by turning material inside and out, backward and forward, I settled on a top and a bottom that together would make (sigh) the perfect wedding dress. Shoshana, dressmaker extraordinaire, drew up an exquisite picture and said she could make it for me for a not-too-exquisite price. She would even include the veil for free. And so I put down a deposit and walked out into the suddenly lovely day to have a little lunch.

Wedding Myth # 36: **Veils are one-size-fits-all.** *The length and style of your veil should match the length and style of your dress (not to mention the size of your head).*

Hiring a designer, or even simply a seamstress who can make a dress from a pattern you've picked out, is often the perfect option for busy brides who may not have a lot of time to shop all over town for the perfect dress. Their prices are usually much lower than the price of a designer dress, with the added perk that your dress will look exactly like you want it to, whether simple, unique, or an exact replica of the one on page fifteen of your local bridal magazine. The best way to find a designer or seamstress is by word of mouth, so don't be shy about asking your friends or family for the name of a reputable seamstress or tailor in the area.

When you buy a dress from a seamstress, you are paying both for her labor and for the materials used in your dress. If you've fallen in love with the style of a dress but the price is above what you've budgeted, ask if there's a similar but less expensive fabric she can use. You should also make certain your seamstress will be able to finish your dress by your wedding date. Get a schedule of the necessary fittings (these can sometimes take up a lot of time, so start your search for a seamstress early), as well as a payment schedule. Most seamstresses require a deposit, payment on completion of the muslin, and final payment on delivery of the dress. In comparing prices with dresses you may see in boutiques and other stores, keep in mind that all alterations are included in a seamstress's price, while a store's fees for alterations can sometimes cost as much as $200 more than the actual dress.

The secret is that fittings and fixings are actually enjoyable. I was engaged for a year and a half before the wedding and, early on, my dress fittings were sometimes the only reminder that I was getting married at all. There was also something amazing about watching the dress, first made from muslin, then from silk, little by little come to resemble the dress of my dreams. And what better way to end a long day at work than by slipping into a beautiful silk dress and being fitted and fussed over?

BRIDAL WAREHOUSES

Bridal warehouses store an enormous number of dresses, some at full price, some at discounts. You may be left on your own to sort through racks of dresses, or you may be assigned a salesperson who will escort you to a private dressing room and bring dresses to you. Many of these bridal warehouses and salons are "full-service" and will schedule fittings and alterations for you, although one bride notes that because warehouses deal with so many brides, it's sometimes difficult to schedule fitting appointments. As with everything else to do with weddings, it's not a bad idea to start your search early. Bridal warehouses also generally stock (or can order) shoes, veils, gloves, and all your other wedding-day accessories. They often sell bridesmaid dresses as well, so round up your bridesmaids and make an afternoon of it.

Wedding Myth #37: **All wedding accessories are necessary.**
Shoes, veils, gloves, scarves, shawls, jewelry, purses, stockings, bustiers, and garters are lovely when they complement your dress, not when they block your guests' view of your dress.

ANYTHING OTHER THAN A WEDDING GOWN

Traditional wedding gowns aren't for you? Great—don't wear one. Erin got married in blue jeans. Tamaki wore a kimono made in her grandparents' hometown in Japan. Susan wore a ski suit. Erica wore a pants suit. Martha and John and their guests rented Victorian period costumes from a local costume store. Layli and Bob were married at a nudist colony and wore nothing at all. It's your wedding—choose something (or nothing!) that makes you feel beautiful, happy, and comfortable.

WEDDING DRESS DOS

Now, for most wedding decisions, I am all for throwing out the rules. However, when it comes to your wedding dress, I find that a few (just a few) are necessary. Unlike other wedding mishaps, if something goes wrong with your dress, you will not be able to just ignore it—mainly because you are going to be in it. With that in mind, make sure you can do the following:

BREATHE This seems obvious, but for some reason, it often isn't. Linda, for instance, let pride get in her way and ordered a dress two sizes too small, confident she would lose weight and her dress would fit. She didn't and the dress didn't. Note: Taking in a dress that is too big is far easier than letting out a dress that is too small. Don't think of ordering a larger dress as a bad thing (most wedding dress sizes run small anyway). Instead, think of breathing as a good thing. I guarantee you'll have a much better chance of making it through the day alive.

MOVE YOUR ARMS When your pastor, priest, or rabbi announces in front of everybody that it's time to kiss the bride, it would be nice if you could reach your arms around your hubby's neck and plant a wet one on him. Hint: You won't be able to if you can't move your arms. You will also be unable to do all sorts of other fun things like hug your wedding guests, throw your bouquet, and dance. The macarena especially requires full use of your arms.

SIT DOWN If you have no plans whatsoever of sitting down in your wedding dress, skip ahead to the next item. However, if you intend to sit down and eat, you will want to make sure your dress cooperates. Many hoop skirts have a tendency to fly straight up, providing wedding guests with a nice view of your lacy new lingerie. And wedding dresses with bustles have a tendency to be difficult to sit on. Consider looping your train over the back of your chair and then re-bustling it for dance hour. (Don't forget to bring along a best friend to your final fitting to figure out how to tie your bustle after the ceremony). Also consider that while a dress may fit perfectly well when you're standing up, you may need just a little more give to sit comfortably. One very embarrassed bride split her dress seams when sitting down for dinner.

WALK Again, this seems obvious, but many brides-to-be become so enamored of their reflections at the bridal salon that they don't consider whether they'll actually be able to make it down the aisle. Take a stroll. Is the dress too heavy, too tight, too long? Or even more important, too big? I know, this sounds silly, but once upon a time there was a bride whose dress was so big, it knocked down all the pew decorations as she walked down the aisle. In the middle of "The Wedding March," she had to stop while guests moved the rest of the decorations out of her way.

GO TO THE BATHROOM BY YOURSELF This rule I actually consider optional. First of all, you're never going to actually be by yourself on your wedding day, so it's just silly. Second of all, most bathrooms weren't invented to accommodate ball gowns (I guess folks just don't wear them as much as they used to) and all of that material can be pretty heavy. Plus, you've just spent round about a year taking off clothes in front of absolute strangers while looking for your dress, so what's left of your modesty probably won't keep you from asking a few best friends to help you out.

GET YOUR DRESS ON AND GET YOUR DRESS OFF Believe it or not, this is actually more difficult than it sounds. It took Sarah's bridesmaids and mother almost two hours to finish buttoning the fifty teeny-tiny buttons that went up the back of her dress. Admittedly, it took her groom far less time to undo them—he simply ripped them off. If your wedding dress has loop-and-hole buttons, bring along a couple of crochet hooks for your friends, and be sure and keep one in your purse for your groom.

PAY FOR YOUR DRESS This may seem a bit confusing, because as I'm sure you already know, there are lots of different dresses out there at lots of different prices. My advice: Look only at dresses you can afford. Sooner or later you will fall in love with one. If you look at dresses you can't afford, you are bound to fall in love with a dress you can't afford and will convince yourself to spend money you don't have. Hint: There are still the shoes and veil and jewelry and lingerie (don't forget the lingerie) to buy. Another hint: Once you've found your dress, stop looking. Otherwise, you will drive your mom, your friends, not to mention yourself, crazy.

THE WEDDING DRESS CONTRACT

Okay, now that you're comfortable with your dress and the price, make sure your contract/receipt includes the following:

- ◆ Dress color, type of material, style number, designer, and/or picture if you're having the dress made.

- ◆ Size and/or your measurements.

- ◆ Total cost.

- ◆ Delivery date and delivery address.

- ◆ Special-order requests.

- ◆ Store's alteration policy. (Will they provide alterations? Are they included in the price of the dress? If not, what are additional charges?)

- Cancellation/refund policies.

- Policy in case of fire or other mishap.

And, last but not least, be sure and work out the specifics of the delivery of your dress. If your dress is being made in one city, your wedding is being held in another city, and you will be taking a plane between the two, you do not, I repeat, you do not want to have to take your dress on the plane with you. Dresses can actually be mailed rather easily, with little in the way of damage other than a slight wrinkle or two. Dresses, however, cannot easily be put on a plane. Take it from Isa, who had to wheel her dress through the airport in a wheelchair (her groom struggling behind her with the rest of the luggage). Take it from me, who had to cram my dress through the security conveyor belt and then squash it into first class's coat closet. Paying a little extra to have your dress shop mail your dress (don't forget to insure it) is a small price to pay for making sure the dress of your dreams arrives *looking* like a dream.

Dressing Everybody Else

There may seem like an unbelievable number of people you are going to need to dress for your wedding, but all of these people will generally fall into one of two categories: girls and boys. Let's start with the girls first, since girls usually tend to care more about what they're wearing than boys do. The boys, on the other hand, could very possibly show up at your wedding in tank tops and jogging shorts if left on their own, so you'll need to take a little time dressing them, too. Your grandmother has waited a long time for this moment; let's not give her a heart attack before you even make it down the aisle.

BRIDESMAIDS

Once upon a time, all bridesmaids wore dresses identical to the bride's. The theory goes that they were trying to protect the bride from evil spirits or from actual live evildoers in the form of marauders who roamed the countryside for the sole purpose of kidnapping brides. Bridesmaids put an end to this tradition just as soon as they realized how costly and dangerous the practice actually was. Much later, it became the tradition for brides to pick out ridiculously expensive and hideously ugly dresses that their bridesmaids would never wear again. This was the bride's way of testing her friendships. If the bridesmaid actually showed up wearing the appropriate (or completely inappropriate) dress, she immediately became a friend for life. Today, the tradition hasn't changed all that much, although not for lack of trying on brides' parts. At some point or another, we all become seriously dedicated to finding a bridesmaid dress for our friends that is actually appropriate. More often than not, however, our efforts fail.

Take my own experience. After umpteen trips to umpteen different department stores, boutiques, fabric stores, bridal salons, and seamstresses, my bridesmaids were still dressless two months before the wedding. At one point, I even threw up my hands and attempted to leave the whole thing to the bridesmaids. Sadly, this did not prove fruitful either. What did prove fruitful was a last-minute trip to Ann Taylor during a spring clearance sale where I miraculously found the perfect dress, on sale, in regular and petite sizes. I immediately bought every dress they had and instructed my mother to do the same at the Ann Taylor stores in Georgia. My sister did likewise in California. Between the three of us, all six bridesmaids were finally suited up in silvery blue sleeveless dresses with nifty embroidery at the top, and after I ordered six pairs of dyed-to-match sandals, their feet looked equally as snazzy. Now, did the girls like the dresses? Yes. Were the dresses comfortable and appropriate for an outdoor reception? Yes. Were the dresses reasonably priced? Yes. Will my bridesmaids ever wear these dresses again? Probably not.

Bridesmaid dresses can be a difficult concept to understand. In theory, you should be able to find a dress that will look relatively good on everyone and that everyone will wear again and again. Every bride rebels against the idea that the dress she has so carefully picked out will hang uselessly in her friends' closets. Unfortunately, this is pretty much a fact. It's also a fact that almost every girl out there has accepted this and has stopped caring. I personally have five bridesmaid dresses hanging in my closet as we speak, and I have a hunch you probably have a couple yourself. Now, did we complain about the dresses when we bought them? Yes. Are we honestly upset with any of the brides over the dresses? No. What is more important than any silly dress is the silly best friend who is going absolutely out of her mind trying to find you one you'll wear again. Besides, I have actually bought a dress or two—without any help from a bride—that I have never worn again.

I would wear any dress in the world for one day if my best friend asked me to. And you probably would, too. So, give up the fight. Pick out whatever dress is easiest and causes the least amount of pain, time, and money to order. Ballerina pink. Peacock blue. Silk. Satin. Suede. Whatever. Your friends love you and whether or not they love their dresses makes absolutely no difference in the world. Just remember that your best friend may be the next one walking down the aisle, and then it will be *her* turn to test *your* friendship.

> *Wedding Myth* # 38: ***All bridesmaids have to wear the same dress.*** *This was the old rule. The new rule is that bridesmaids' dresses should be comfortable and appropriate and make the bridesmaids happy. If your bridesmaids are capable of following the new rule on their own, let them. They're happy, you're happy.*

With all of this in mind, you have several options for picking out the perfect bridesmaid dress that your friends will, nevertheless, probably never wear again. If your wedding is a formal affair and your bridesmaids will be in need of long formal dresses or evening gowns, a bridal salon is your best bet. They have racks and catalogs full of full-length dresses that come in a variety of styles and colors—and most bridesmaid dress companies are so fashion forward these days, the dresses are actually rather attractive. If any of your bridesmaids live in the same city as you, drag them along one rainy Saturday to the local salon and play dress up. These friends can have their measurements taken at the shop, while friends who live out of town can call in their measurements. Tip: Make sure these are real measurements. Many a bridesmaid who has faked her measurements has wound up with a dress that she could not even begin to fake getting into. Bridesmaid dresses, like wedding dresses, run small. Now is no time for vanity. After all, everybody's best friends here, right? Right. Get real measurements.

Ordering dresses from a bridal salon has many benefits. All of the dresses will arrive at the same place at the same time, and bridesmaids can have alterations done at the bridal shop up to and including the day of the wedding if necessary. However, if your bridesmaids are scattered across the country, you might opt to have the dresses mailed directly to them. This way, any catastrophes (wrong color, wrong size) can be discovered well before the wedding and each bridesmaid can have alterations done on her own. If the dresses will be delivered to the bridal salon, ask if alterations are included in the price of the dress or if there is an extra fee. Also ask for a payment schedule. Often, half of the price of a dress is due when you place the order and the remainder when the dress arrives. This is a nice way of spreading out the cost for your friends, since most bridal salons can be expensive.

Many boutiques and seamstresses also specialize in bridesmaid dresses and often offer funkier and more creative styles. They also offer the same services as a bridal salon, including taking measurements, arranging for alterations, and sometimes providing catalogs of matching shoes and accessories. Prices can be as high as bridal salons, and, sometimes, more so. Be sure and check a seamstress's references and ask to see samples of her work. Jessica didn't, and her bridesmaids wound up with dresses that were supposed to look exactly the same but didn't. The mismatched and completely mis-sewn dresses also smelled rather strongly of something other than cigarette smoke. Sometimes "funky" can be a little too funky. Even if you're buying your dresses off the rack, you may still want to line up a reliable seamstress for last-minute alterations. My cousin, for instance, flew in for the wedding from Italy and needed to have alterations done two days before the wedding.

For casual bridesmaid dresses, department stores and other smaller chain stores offer a wide selection of styles and prices. Many of these stores are national chains and bridesmaids in different cities can be on the lookout for a stellar dress at a stellar price. A salesperson at one store can put dresses on hold at other stores as well. And if the perfect dress you pick out a year before the wedding turns out to be not quite so perfect, you can always exchange it for another dress closer to your wedding date. You may even decide to head to a fabric store and pick out a fabric and a fabulous dress pattern. Or, simply pick out a fabric color and have everyone either buy or sew their own dresses. Also consider that black isn't just for funerals anymore. More and more brides are having bridesmaids pick out simple black cocktail dresses in whatever style is most flattering to that bridesmaid (and several bridesmaids even report wearing these again!).

MOTHERS

Dresses for mothers are oftentimes as difficult to find as bridesmaids' dresses. There's no real reason for this except for the fact that when it comes to weddings, difficulty always seems to be in vogue. For my sister's wedding, for example, my mother purchased somewhere around four or five dresses. She couldn't make up her mind. So when my future mother-in-law and stepmother-in-law asked me what my mother would be wearing to the wedding, I told them that I honestly had no idea. It is customary for the groom's mother to consult with the bride's mother on attire, so styles, lengths, and colors are similar, pictures look nice, and no one is embarrassed. But since I knew my mother probably wouldn't decide on a dress until a week or even a day before the wedding, I gave my mothers-in-law the thumbs-up to go ahead on their own, and things turned out perfectly. All three dresses were shades of blue, the pictures look nice, and no one was embarrassed.

Now, I have heard of many, many mothers-of-the-bride who get it into their heads to wear a white or champagne-colored dress (one mother-in-law showed up in a white, skintight, sleeveless prom dress). The daughters of these mothers have come up with the theory that their mothers are trying to steal the limelight and, in fact, want to be the bride themselves. Maybe this is true. Maybe it isn't. In any case, I'm not sure any of the fights I've heard described over this issue are worth the end result. (The mother wears white anyway and the daughter never talks to her again. The mother doesn't wear white but never speaks to her daughter again.) I'd venture a guess that even if your mother wears white, she isn't going to be mistaken for the bride. A waiter or two may be confused, but certainly not the two people who matter most: you and your groom. Considering the fact that you will have just gotten married (yeeee-haw!), would it really matter if *all* of your wedding guests showed up wearing white? And if you're not even planning on wearing a white wedding dress yourself, consider the problem solved. (Unless, of course, your mother decides to wear the exact same navy suit as you. Again, difficulty is in vogue, so be prepared for anything.)

FLOWER GIRLS

Flower girl dresses are adorable. Actually, little girl dresses are adorable, period, which is why our flower girl's mother brought home seven dresses for Emily to model. The entire family was in attendance and Emily had all day to strut her stuff. Emily is three years old and had only one requirement: The dress should twirl. The rest of us had a different, but equally important, requirement: The dress shouldn't expose anything shocking while she twirled. Emily is moody—she may or may not be in the mood to wear underwear, so we had to take precautions. The winning dress had a spectacular skirt with petal-like panels of wispy white fabric interspersed with strategically placed purple ones, making it an excellent pick. It also didn't hurt that Emily looked like the cutest little fairy in the world as she twirled across the room and dutifully practiced her pigeon-toed "flower girl walk." Her mother found an adorable headband to match the dress and brought along three pairs of shoes or so, once again taking into account a three-year-old's moods.

Not all flower girls are three years old, but most are moody. They will love being a flower girl. They will hate being a flower girl. They will love their dress. They will hate their dress. The dress will be the most comfortable dress they've ever put on. The dress will be scratchy, itchy, stiff, tight (i.e., the most uncomfortable dress they've ever put on). My vote is to leave finding a dress up to the flower girl's parents. Let the mother or father know what your colors are (pastel, primary) and have them find a dress that's appropriate for the occasion, their budget, and their little girl's mood. That's one less person you'll have to worry about dressing—and one less person you'll have to worry about pleasing.

GROOM

Your wedding day is every bit as much your groom's dream as it is yours, so while you may be tempted to plan your groom's outfit right down to his pant cuffs, it might be best to let him dress himself (after all, he doesn't get any say about what you wear). In fact, your groom may be more of a clotheshorse than you are. John's brand-new, custom-made tuxedo, for instance, was more elaborate (and expensive) than Sarah's simple silk sheath wedding dress. And Michael, although a bit more budget-conscious, showed up at his wedding with two different shirts in case he changed his mind at the last minute—or sweated through one before the ceremony started.

Of course, your groom may be completely lost when it comes to fashion, so by all means offer your help. To stand out from his groomsmen, he may want to pick out a different color or style cummerbund and bow tie, and perhaps even a different color shirt. Brian, for instance, wore a navy suit to contrast with his groomsmen's navy jackets and khaki pants and picked out a fabulous light blue woven shirt and tie. For a formal wedding, your groom might choose to wear a silk vest or an ascot. Steve wore a morning suit for his early wedding and still talks about how cool he looked. And don't forget accessories. The night before the wedding, give him a unique pair of antique cuff links or some new silk monogrammed undies. Have your florist create a special boutonniere (perhaps the flower he brought you on your first date?). If your groom is feeling especially sentimental, go ahead and let him lace up that favorite pair of basketball shoes (and feel free to wear yours, too). The only requirement here is that your groom feel as special (and comfortable) on your wedding day as you do.

GROOMSMEN

Brian's and my wedding was in June, in Georgia. Our reception was outside, so making our groomsmen wear tuxedoes seemed cruel. Although Brian's friends actually said they liked dressing up at weddings and hinted that they would prefer a tuxedo, most of them had never been to Georgia in June, when it could easily be ninety degrees. So, just to be on the safe side, we opted to suit our guys in more casual attire. Khaki pants, white shirts, navy blazers, brown shoes and belts, and a spectacular navy tie with white daisylike flowers that Brian picked out as each groomsman's gift.

Wedding Myth # 39: **All groomsmen have to wear tuxedos.**
If your wedding is a formal, evening, winter wedding at the Plaza, probably. Otherwise, think about how much more often your guys will wear a new suit. Khaki pants and navy blazers in the summer. Black or gray pinstripe suits in the winter. Classy and comfortable.

If you do decide to go the formal route, simply send your grooms-men to their closets to pull out those tuxedoes they bought way back when Cousin John got bar mitzvahed, or send them to a local tuxedo shop. Keep in mind the formality of your event and even mention to the salesperson what time of day your wedding will be held. He can help you with everything from the jacket and pants to bow ties (including instructions on how to tie them), cummerbunds (how tight is too tight?), shoes (how not to slip down the aisle), and all those other fun accessories like studs, cuff links, vests, and handkerchiefs. Above all, make sure they're comfortable. No need to make enemies of your future husband's friends this early in the game.

RING BEARER

Little boy clothes are just as cute as little girl clothes, but don't expect your three-year-old ring bearer to twirl around in his new frock. You might, however, want to prepare yourself for a little bit of twisting—of his tie. Whether your ring bearer's outfit includes a necktie or a bow tie, remember that this is probably the youngster's first time out with something around his neck. And he might not like it. Expect him to pose for pictures and then deposit the tie somewhere handy: his mother's purse, for instance. Again, it seems best to leave the dressing of children to their parents. That way, the offending tie is all their fault—and not yours.

One note regarding the wee ones: Line up all the children in the wedding before the ceremony and make them go to the bathroom whether they want to or not. Rhonda's ring bearer decided halfway through the ceremony to go sit on his mother's lap—and then proceeded to pee all over her. A little bit of aggravation before the wedding can save you a whole lot of aggravation during the wedding.

DADS

Dads are usually low-key about their wedding day getup. If the groomsmen are wearing tuxes, they'll don a tux. If the guys are wearing suits, they'll whip out a suit. Of course, if you think Dad's feeling a bit left out of all the dressing games, pick out a special tie just for him (and don't forget to tell him you love him).

GUESTS

Most male wedding guests are not worried in the slightest about their wedding attire. Most female guests, however, are not only worried about their wedding attire, but will become slightly hysterical. This phenomenon occurs round about a week or two before the wedding when they realize that all those really cute clothes they thought they had hanging in their closets have suddenly disappeared. To help out your guests, give your mother and one or two best friends the lowdown on appropriate wedding attire and have them spread the word.

For instance, at my sister's summer wedding by the river, she thought it would be lovely to have all the girls decked out in hats. My mother passed along the request and everybody showed up in hats of every color and variety. The pictures are amazing. If you are having a black-tie or theme wedding, you might include dressing instructions in your reception invitation. One creative bride who was hosting a formal, but not at all stuffy, evening wedding had these instructions engraved on her invitations: "Black tie and tiaras optional." She even provided plastic tiaras for guests who didn't bring their own. Dressing up for weddings can be a lot of fun—why not let your guests join in?

PART III

Right Before

Registering

EENIE MEENIE MINIE MO

Registering for wedding gifts may strike some newly engaged couples as a bit odd. I mean, it's like telling people what to buy you. Isn't that rude? Yes and no. People are going to buy you gifts anyway. They love you and would like nothing more than to get you something you'll love. They would also like getting something you love to be easy. That's where registering comes in. Instead of guessing what you and your beloved's taste in crystal, china, and towels might be, or trying to ascertain what your favorite colors are, your friends and family can simply head to the store of your choice and pick out something you've already decided you love and want forever. They are happy. You are happy. Everyone's happy.

Registering, however, does mean using your head. Consider what you already have and don't have and what you will really, honestly use. If you already have a perfectly good toaster, don't register for a new one. If you don't even have a dining room table and aren't sure when you'll be getting one, fine china probably isn't going to come in handy anytime soon. On the other hand, once you do finally get a table, consider whether you'll be able to afford china on your own. Even if you won't be hosting a dinner party for twelve in the near future, it can be nice to pull out a couple of place settings, light a few candles, and have an elegant picnic for two right on your living room floor. Fine china is just one of those things that says, "We're *married*." Nice, huh?

How do you know where to register? Ask a best friend whose taste you admire where she registered. Shop around at your local department stores or fine jewelry stores (which often carry china as well as silverware). Note which stores carry the patterns of china and crystal you are interested in, as well as a wide variety of linens and other housewares. Or, if you're more into fishing gear than fine china, check out your local sporting goods store. Find out what other states the store is located in and ask if they have an 800 number or a web site for easy ordering (some stores may even have cross-registries with other stores). Other questions you may want to ask include: Will the store ship gifts to your home or will you need to pick them up? If they ship, does the store pay for shipping or does the guest? What is the store's return policy? Can you return a gift for store credit or cash? How long do you have to return a gift? How can you check and update your registry—by phone, e-mail, or web site? Will they alert you if any of your registry items are discontinued? Will you receive a discount if you finish your registry yourself?

Whew, okay, now how in the world do you actually register? Not to worry. It's not difficult. In fact, registering is almost exactly like playing one of your very favorite games from childhood. Really? Yep. Read on.

HOW TO REGISTER: CANDYLAND FOR ADULTS

Something wonderful has happened in Candyland! Now there is a brand-new adult version. Instead of visiting such magical places as the Peanut Brittle House, the Gumdrop Mountains, and the Molasses Swamp, you will travel to the Wild World of Wares, the Land of Linens, Appliance Alley, and Electronic Avenue. Gone are the lollipops, licorice sticks, and lemon drops, and in their places are new types of candy: mochachino makers, salad spinners, and stovetop grills. But remember, you don't win Candyland by having the most candy.

The challenge for you and your groom is simply to find your way through the maze of candy and home again, still in one piece and still completely (or at least mostly) in love.

CONTENTS

- ◆ Registry form/s. Registry forms provide spaces for you and/or your partner to record gift bar codes or sku numbers (those numerical codes on price tags), descriptions, quantities, and prices. Registry forms do not, however, necessarily provide enough room to record all of the required information, so be prepared to write really, really tiny.

- ◆ One clipboard. Clipboards are very useful for clipping registry forms to but can be quite dangerous if used to hit another player on the head.

- ◆ Laser gun. A laser gun is a small electronic device that, by means of a thin red beam, identifies and records the bar codes on all items in a store. Instead of manually writing down the bar codes or sku numbers of the gifts you choose, you simply "zap" the bar code with the laser gun, thereby registering more quickly and accurately. A bridal registry salesperson can then download the laser gun information into their computer and spit out a handy-dandy registry list for you and all of your wedding guests. Not all stores have laser guns, but many do. Laser guns can be a lot of fun. Laser guns can also cause a lot of fights. Since this has a tendency to slow down play, I have devised three rather essential rules regarding laser gun use for you and your groom:

1. DON'T YELL AT YOUR GROOM. If you yell at your groom for mishandling the laser gun or criticize his laser gun technique, he will get very depressed and probably want to go home. He will not want to go registering ever again. You will never finish picking out crystal. You will wind up with no towels. So, go ahead and let him mishandle the laser gun. He gets the gun; you get the towels.

2. IT IS OKAY TO LIE TO YOUR GROOM. It is okay to lie and tell him that the next store has a laser gun as well. He will be sad when he finds out the truth, but he will still be on such a high from using the laser gun at the first store that he will somehow survive the disappointment.

3. ENJOY YOUR GROOM. He is not zapping everything in the store simply to make you crazy. He is zapping everything in the store simply because he can. He was listening (when you weren't) to the salesperson who said you could make changes to your registry at the end of the day. And this is true. Relax. If your boy zaps ten different china patterns, you can take off nine of them. I promise. Plus, this is probably the most excited you will ever see your groom throughout the whole wedding planning process. It's also probably the only time you'll ever get to hear him say: "Oh no, are we really finished shopping?" Having your ass zapped is a small price to pay to see your groom so happy.

PLAYERS

In the original version of Candyland, the game was played with two to four players. In the adult version, you may choose to play alone (which can sometimes make for quicker playing time) or with a partner.

HOW TO PLAY THE GAME

Proceed by yourself or with your partner to your registry store of choice. Pick up all required playing pieces from your store's bridal registry, along with instructions, which may be written or verbal or both. Skip (arm in arm is preferable although not required) through each department choosing gifts that (1) you think you will want for a very long time and (2) you think your guests will want to give you.

Wedding Myth #40: **Everyone can afford to buy you everything you want.** *They can't. Choose gifts in all price ranges so all of your guests can give you something you'll like.*

Playing at different times of day can often result in quicker—or longer—playing times. Playing when no one else is playing (i.e., times when the store is less crowded) will prove faster, easier, and much, much nicer. You might also choose to play the on-line version, in which moving forward can be as quick or as slow as clicking a button. If you are playing at more than one store, you may decide to play a series of games. You might also decide to play the Saturday afternoon marathon game (good luck).

If you are playing the game with a partner, the goal is to finish the game together. This means you cannot leave your partner in electronics while you sneak away to linens. Of course, if playing together means you are likely never to finish the game—or wind up married, for that matter—you may amend the rules as you see fit.

After you have completed skipping through all departments (or all the departments you have time for in that particular round) return to the store's bridal registry with all game pieces. Your bridal registry will compile a list of each and every gift you have written down or zapped with the laser gun, allowing you and/or your partner to make any necessary changes. The store will then mail a completed registry list to your home or perhaps even give you a fancy computerized list right then and there. Whichever the case, skip to store's exit and live happily ever after.

DEPARTMENTS

There are many new playing spaces called departments scattered across the board of Candyland for Adults. You have the option of landing on all of these spaces, some of them, or none of them, depending on your mood and the amount of available closet and shelf space in your future house or apartment. These departments include:

The Wild World of Wares

In the Wild World of Wares you will find many different types of wares: dishware, stemware, barware, flatware, kitchenware, cookware, and bakeware. This will be confusing until you realize they are all basically things that go in your kitchen.

DISHWARE Dishware refers to everyday dishes and fine china. Everyday dishes are the dishes you plan on using every day and don't mind too terribly if one gets scratched in the dishwasher or if you break one because you don't have a dishwasher. Fine china refers to dishes made of bone or fine porcelain china. These dishes are more expensive and are used on only very special occasions such as Thanksgiving dinners, dinner parties, intimate dinners for two, and when all of your everyday dishes are dirty. While many types of fine china can now be put in the dishwasher, others still need to be washed by hand, so be sure your groom-to-be is willing to wash dishes if you choose delicate china. Moms across America suggest registering for twelve five-piece place settings of both everyday and fine china, as well as twelve soup/salad bowls and matching serving pieces.

STEMWARE/BARWARE Stemware (wineglasses, champagne flutes, water goblets) and barware (highballs, lowballs, shot glasses) are fancy words for glasses. Glasses can be made out of either everyday, hard-to-break glass or not-for-everyday, easy-to-break crystal. Moms suggest registering for twelve glasses of each type of glass.

FLATWARE Flatware is a term used to describe your eating utensils. Some flatware comes in silver (often called sterling) and is very elegant, very beautiful, very expensive, and very difficult to clean. Silverware cannot go in the dishwasher and must be hand-washed and then polished with a special silver cloth. The other type of flatware is made of stainless steel and can be just as beautiful and elegant, but is less expensive and much, much easier to clean. You might register for a set of one or the other or both. Traditionally, brides-to-be keep a set of each. However, more and more brides are opting for stainless ware so they can put their utensils in the dishwasher and be done with it. Once again, Moms suggest registering for twelve place settings as well as various serving utensils.

KITCHENWARE/COOKWARE/BAKEWARE These are all things you cook with, bake with, or otherwise use to spruce up your kitchen counter. Register for as many as you see fit.

The Land of Linens

In the Land of Linens you will find linens for every part of your home. Bed linens go in your bedroom (three sets of sheets for each bed in your home is the general rule). Table linens go in your kitchen and dining room (choose an assortment of tablecloths, place mats, and napkins). Bath linens go in your bathroom (eight bath towels, hand towels, and facecloths should do it).

Appliance Alley/Electronic Avenue

These departments are full of nifty electronic things for your kitchen and home. (Note: The niftier the appliance looks, the harder it will be to use.) One of each item is probably enough.

> *Wedding Myth* #41: **You have to register for gifts.** *A nice alternative is to have guests give to a charity of your choice. On such a special day, why not share your blessings with others?*

HOW TO WIN THE GAME

You win the game when you finish registering, turn in all game pieces, and go home. Winning has absolutely nothing to do with whether or not you actually get all of the candy you have just registered for. Candy, in fact, has little to do with the game of Candyland at all. Your marriage, however, does, which is why the adult version of Candyland was invented in the first place: to see if couples contemplating marriage could successfully navigate their way through the many departments, dilemmas, even disputes that registering involves. Congratulations on winning Candyland and best wishes for a happy marriage!

AFTER THE GAME

All right, you've finished the game. Now what? Well, more games of course! First up is:

The Waiting Game

After completing your game of Candyland, wait around for a bit. After a while, your store will send you a note informing you that you have a present to be picked up or may actually mail the gift directly to you. Ideally, you'll be able to receive gifts at home. Otherwise, you will need to pick up gifts at your local post office. Hint: Drive your largest car. Even if someone buys you a cake slicer, it will come in a box big enough to hold your wedding cake. You may also receive cards informing you that your gift is on back order and will be delivered as soon as it is available (which may or may not be when you were planning on using it). You may choose to let gift boxes pile up and open them after your wedding or you may choose to open them as they arrive. In either case, you will need to play this very next game:

The Tracking Game

Remember that box of index cards with each guest's name and address? Find it. Write on each card what gift a guest gave you and check it off when you've mailed a thank-you. If you decide not to open presents until after the wedding, have someone keep a list of each gift as well as whom it was from as you open each one. Record the information on the appropriate index cards later. Also be sure and record any shower or engagement presents you receive.

> *Wedding Myth* # 42: **Thanking people in person for their gifts is sufficient.** *Thanking people for their gifts does not count unless it is done in ink on paper through the mail. You do, however, get extra points for thanking people in person.*

The Thank-You Game

The thank-you game is not optional. Game contents include thank-you notes, envelopes, stamps, and a pen. This game goes much (much) quicker with two players. While there are no laser guns, the game is not hard and can be a lot of fun. It gives you the opportunity to thank your guests for not only their gifts, but for everything they've done for you over the years—and especially over the last few months. Writing thank-you notes is also an excellent opportunity for you and your groom to recount (since everybody else may very well be tired of talking about it) all of the wonderful details of your wedding day.

Primping 101

HOW TO MAKE YOURSELF BEAUTIFUL

Every bride dreams of looking beautiful on her wedding day. The perfect hair, perfect makeup, perfect skin, perfect fingernails, perfect toenails, perfectly shaved legs, perfectly shaped arms. Primping has a tendency to turn into a bit of an obsession. Take Anna, who, desperate for a wedding-day glow, dreamt up the idea to rub Vaseline all over her face. And Phyllis, who spent several months (and more than several bucks) in pursuit of the perfect shade of lipstick. I had my own dreams—literally. Every night for a month I dreamt about my hair: short hair, long hair, dirty hair, wet hair, dry hair, not-ready-in-time hair. In one dream I was standing in the middle of a field, my wedding dress billowing around me as my bridesmaids curled my hair with dozens of curling irons.

These dreams, I decided in amusement, meant absolutely nothing. As it turned out, I was wrong. They meant absolutely everything, which brings me to my very first tip for looking beautiful on your wedding day: Pay attention to your dreams. They are the little hints telling you how you want to feel on your wedding day, and, in my case, turned out to be important clues to an impending disaster. So take note: Do you dream of floating down your grandparents' staircase with nothing more than lightly lined lips and slightly flushed cheeks? Or is it your dream to dazzle your groom with a little glitter (all the better to match your tiara) at your evening wedding?

All brides—and their dreams—will be different, but whether you dream of wearing lots of makeup or no makeup, wearing your hair up or down (or a combination of both), chances are you're looking for a little bit of advice for looking beautiful and, more important, *feeling* beautiful on your wedding day. With this in mind, I've gathered a few rules from several makeup artists, guidelines from a couple of hairstylists, and a ton of tips from brides on stocking an emergency wedding-day beauty kit. Because pimples will pop up, hairs will split, fall, or worse, fall out (more on this in a bit), and just like for any other wedding-day emergency, you'll want to be prepared.

Wedding Myth #43: **The more makeup you wear, the prettier you'll look.** *The more makeup you wear, the sillier you'll look—in photographs and in person. Makeup should be used to highlight your beauty, not mask it.*

MAKEUP

The good news about makeup is that there's a lot of help out there for brides who want to look beautiful on their wedding day. If you're planning on doing your makeup yourself, take this opportunity to visit a cosmetics counter at a local department store. Most makeup counters offer complimentary consultations for brides, in which they determine your skin type and color, help you begin a personalized beauty regimen, and teach you the proper way to apply each product—skills that are good for your wedding day as well as the rest of your life.

To give your products a chance to work, make an appointment three weeks to six months before your wedding. Choose a consultant whose own makeup you like, and be sure and share how you want to feel on the big day (natural, glamorous), as well as giving her a description of your wedding: time of day, time of year, type of wedding (casual, formal), location (outside, inside), and color scheme. Many makeup counters also offer skin consultations for your bridesmaids and mom, so bring them along for a full day of primping and pampering. And if you're not sure you'll be able to re-create the consultant's look on your own, ask a friend who's a wizard with a makeup brush to pay close attention, and have her do your makeup on your wedding day. Or hire the consultant herself—for a fee, most are available to do makeup for both you and your bridesmaids.

You might also choose to hire a makeup artist for your wedding day. Although more expensive than doing your makeup yourself, hiring a professional ensures you won't make any beauty blunders yourself. Makeup artists are also more experienced with applying makeup that will look good in photographs, contouring and blending each product for a perfectly subtle look, and making sure features such as your eyebrows and lashes don't fade away. Makeup artists are familiar with the lighting of different settings: a candlelight ceremony, for instance, or an outdoor garden party. They'll know how to get your makeup to last for the six or more hours you'll be wearing it on your wedding day, and they're geniuses at taking care of pesky pimples, blotchy skin, or any other problem that may pop up on your wedding day.

Makeup and makeup artists may seem extravagant, especially considering all the money you're spending on flowers and favors and food (and you should never be pressured into buying products you know you don't need). But here's a hint: If you don't feel beautiful on your wedding day, you're not going to care about the flowers or the favors or the food. It's one of those little bridal quirks that, if the bride feels ugly, everything else looks ugly, too. So, if you can, spend a little less on the favors and a little more on your face. After all, you've just spent a lot of time and money putting together a fabulous outfit: your dress, veil, shoes, gloves, and that lacy, racy lingerie. Now is not the time to start scrimping. Either spend the time—visiting a makeup counter, practicing with a friend, taking a makeup course—or the money—hiring a professional makeup artist—to guarantee you look as beautiful as your dreams. And don't forget your fingernails, toenails, legs, and arms. All body parts need a bit of TLC before your wedding day.

Whatever makeup option you choose, there are a few things you should know—about preparing your skin for your wedding day, about steering clear of serious beauty blunders, about choosing a wedding-day look that's right for you. The following are tips I've gathered from makeup artists, cosmetic consultants, even a bride or two on what steps to take—and not to take—for making sure your makeup is perfect.

Makeup Dos

- If you're prone to breakouts or other skin troubles, visit a dermatologist several months before your wedding.

- Have a facial done a month before your wedding, and then follow up with another two weeks before your wedding day.

- Moisturize lips for the perfect wedding-day pucker.

- Your eyebrows frame the rest of your face—have them shaped and plucked a week before your wedding.

- Pick one or two features to highlight: your lips, your eyes. Cheeks will be naturally flushed the day of your wedding anyway.

- Blend makeup well. Obvious contrasts in color, dark blush, for example, will be glaring in photographs.

- Matte your face with powder to prevent shine, and remember your throat and back.

- Curl eyelashes to make them stand out and coat with extra waterproof mascara (or consider having eyelashes tinted for the day for a no-streaking guarantee).

- Apply lipstick that lasts. First apply lip balm, then lipstick, blot, reapply lipstick, line with lip liner, one more application of lipstick, final blotting.

- Wear a button-down shirt while having your hair and makeup done (so you don't have to pull the shirt over your head when changing into your dress).

- Have a friend check for stray lipstick on teeth and mascara flakes on your cheeks before you walk down the aisle.

- Carry extra lipstick, mascara, and powder to freshen up throughout the day.

- Get plenty of sleep and drink lots of water.

- Exercise for a natural, healthy glow.

- Be yourself.

Makeup Don'ts

- No self-tanners the day of your wedding. Finish up all self-tans—and real tans—one to two weeks before your wedding. Both have a tendency to make your skin splotchy, and self-tanners have been known to rub off on wedding dresses.

- No facials, exfoliating, or use of alpha hydroxy products the day of your wedding. All irritate skin, which may be irritated from stress already.

- Don't get out the ice. For puffy eyes and undereye circles use cold compresses soaked in chamomile tea. By using ice you risk breaking capillaries in your face.

- Absolutely do not pluck your eyebrows the day of your wedding. This can leave red, irritated bumps.

- No popping pimples. Dot blemishes with Visene to get the red out and pat (don't rub) with a light, yellowish concealer. Apply foundation and set with loose powder.

- No black eyes: Avoid oily eyeliners and dark eye shadows.

- No black lips: Don't overline lips with dark liner.

- Don't go overboard on powder, which can stick in the creases of your face, especially around the eyes.

- Don't overtouch your face. Your fingers have natural oils on them that you don't want on your face. Use brushes, Q-Tips, or sponges.

- Don't stay up all night the night before the wedding. This will only stress you—and your skin—out.

- Don't go trendy—go classic.

Wedding-Day Emergency Kit

Even when following the rules, troubles may occur. But not to worry, you'll be more than prepared for even the smallest disaster with this tried-and-true wedding-day emergency kit.

- Nail file and nail polish: clear for runs in your stockings and colored to touch up your nails.

- Extra pair of stockings (for when nail polish isn't enough).

- Bobby pins and safety pins.

- Hairbrush and hair spray (depending on how many bridesmaids you have, you may want to bring along a couple of bottles).

- Antistatic spray (good for clingy bridesmaids' dresses as well as flyaway hair).

- Extra lipstick (give a tube to your best lady, your groom, your mother, just so you can touch up wherever and whenever you want).

- Pressed powder (for your face) and baby powder (to sprinkle over your deodorant for heavy-duty sweat control).

- Concealer, waterproof mascara, and compact mirror.

- Deodorant.

- Soap and shampoo (if you're showering away from home, you'll want products your skin and hair are used to).

- Hair dryer (good for drying both hair and spills).

- Travel steamer (for all of those wrinkles you didn't notice before).

- Cotton swabs/cotton balls.

- Tissues.

- Tampons.

- Dental floss (great for cleaning up teeth after nibbling on a cookie—without serious damage to lipstick).

- Breath freshener (homeopathic stress mints do double duty on both breath and brains).

- Perfume.

- Stain remover (Shout wipes are portable and priceless for removing spills from your wedding dress).

- Club soda (may work on spills, too).

- White chalk and Wite-Out (for when stain remover and club soda don't work).

- Prethreaded needle and scissors (dresses and veils and trains are made out of fabric, which means they can tear, which means you need to be prepared).

- Masking tape (when there's no time to sew).

- Sandpaper (scuff bottoms of yours and bridesmaids shoes so no one slips down the aisle).

- Hand lotion (moisturizes dry skin and ensures your wedding ring will slide right on).

- Snacks.

- Bottled water.

- Cell phone (for when you need to call in help).

- Antacid.

- Advil.

- Benadryl (for a sudden case of the hives).

- Hydrocortisone cream (good for hives and other skin irritations).

- Paper bag (for breathing exercises).

- Asthma inhaler (for more serious breathing problems).

- Swiss army knife (hey, you never know).

HAIR

Most brides are at least a little apprehensive when it comes to getting their hair cut for their wedding. What if their hair winds up too short? Too long? Too dark? Too blonde? Despite all of my wacky dreams, however, I wasn't worried in the slightest. Sally, an absolute genius hairstylist, has been cutting my hair for over two years now and has the uncanny ability to cut my hair long or short and still keep me smiling. Plus, I had dutifully scheduled my haircut exactly ten days before the wedding, just like all of the wedding magazines, books, and planners suggested (human hair, evidently, needs at least ten days to recover from the shock of being cut). Thus, I was completely confident when Sally and I had the following conversation:

SALLY: So, are we doing a short summer do?
ME: Yep, it's for the wedding.
SALLY: Whose wedding?
ME: Mine!
SALLY: Oh, that's right! Yikes, I'm cutting your hair for your wedding! Ack. Is there anything we should talk about?
ME: Well, you haven't messed up my hair yet.

Five minutes later, my very worst nightmare came true and I was bald.

Now, there are a few things to be learned from this story. *Wait, you were really bald?* Yep. Bald. *What in the world did you do?* We'll get to that. First, the lessons:

LESSON NUMBER ONE Know your hair. If you have thick hair, do not think you are going to miraculously wake up on the morning of your wedding with thin hair. If you have thin hair, you are not going to wake up with thick hair. Curly hair will not become straight. Straight hair will not become curly. Long hair can be cut off, but my advice is not to try anything brand new for your wedding. Some brides-to-be have done this with great success, but in my book it's tempting fate. Short hair, of course, can be grown long, provided you have enough time. Many brides-to-be with visions of French twists start growing their hair the minute a ring hits their finger. Short hair, however, cannot become long overnight or even in two weeks (I promise). And, if you're prone to disastrous haircuts (my first one occurred at the ripe age of five), don't expect your wedding haircut to be any different.

LESSON NUMBER TWO Talk about your hair. Knowing your hair also means *talking* about your hair. Obviously, "you haven't messed up my hair yet" is not quite enough information for a hairstylist to go on. Leave nothing to chance. Explain in detail to whoever will be styling or cutting your hair (professional hairstylist, mother, best friend) exactly what you want your hair to look like. Bring in pictures from magazines or even a photograph of your hair at its most fabulous. Be sure and share how you want to feel as a bride (pretty versus punky) and any fears you may have about your hair on the big day (wind, rain, humidity, tidal waves). Describe the style of your wedding dress and the time of day and location of both your ceremony and reception sites. You will also want to bring along your veil and headpiece so your hairstylist can practice putting in all those bobby pins and you can practice taking them out. Or, if you're not the type to wear a veil, consider the sophisticated look of a tiara, or go "all natural," tucking tiny, fragrant flower blossoms into your hair.

LESSON NUMBER THREE Take care of your hair. Taking care of your hair means taking the time to have your hair done right. If you can, schedule three appointments: a play date, a practice date, and a performance date. This will give your hairstylist enough time to play with your hair until you pick the absolutely perfect hairstyle, practice it until she can re-create it effortlessly (snap a Polaroid photo so you both remember exactly what it looks like), and then perform it flawlessly on the big day. Schedule your play date approximately a month before your wedding, your practice date ten days before your wedding (your hairstylist will both cut and style your hair), and your performance date the day of your wedding. If you're coloring your hair, schedule an appointment six weeks before your wedding date and another appointment two weeks before your wedding for touch-ups.

A week before your wedding, decide where to meet for your wedding-day appointment—at the hair salon, your house, the church—and make sure to leave plenty of time. Give your hairstylist a schedule of your wedding day: makeup appointment, start of photographs, start of ceremony, and ask if she's available to style your wedding party as well. Although some of your bridesmaids may feel more comfortable doing their own hair, many may see your wedding as an opportunity to do something different and special. (Do something special yourself and pick up this expense for your bridesmaids.)

> *Wedding Myth* #44: **Your groom will not marry you if your hair doesn't look perfect.** *Your groom will marry you no matter what your hair looks like. For one thing, he's too busy worrying about whether or not his own hair looks perfect to even notice yours.*

Okay. So was I really bald? Well, not exactly bald, but my hair was very, very short, shorter than I've ever worn it before in my entire life, and I had absolutely no hair to attach my veil to or to swing around while dancing. What in the world did I do? First, I cried. Then I came to my senses and did what any bald bride would do: I tried hair extensions. Unfortunately, my hairstylist wasn't particularly skilled at attaching hair extensions, so I went home and cried again. Then I tried a hairpiece. This didn't work either.

What did work was a trip to my mother's super-duper hairstylist extraordinaire who, moved by my tears, whipped into action and applied all sorts of groovy hair products that made me look like I had more hair than I did. She twisted and pulled and styled and restyled and took pictures and more pictures until I had what appeared to be hair on my head, a veil that stayed in place, and even more astonishing, a smile on my face. Of course it didn't hurt that a few of the folks at the hair salon happened to mention that I looked like Audrey Hepburn. What bride could ask for more?

The point of the story is that accidents do happen. For instance, what if you, too, wind up bald? What if a pimple pops up, your bubble flip falls, a nail breaks, or five new freckles suddenly appear from nowhere? Well, you could throw yourself on your bed, cry, and reschedule the entire wedding, but a far better solution is to accept your baldness. Make peace with your pimple. Honestly, nobody thought I was bald, and nobody will notice your pimple.

Plus, and here's a promise, dressed in the wedding gown (or suit or sari) of your dreams, you will feel spectacular no matter what the hair on your head or those freckles on your face are doing.

Details

THE LITTLE THINGS THAT COUNT

So far, this book has been all about planning your wedding, from the ceremony to the reception, and picking out the details to make every aspect special. Your mother's heirloom cake topper. A reading from your favorite poem. The lace veil you bought in Brussels when you were nine years old. Specially packaged bubbles for your getaway. And, of course, something old, something new, something borrowed, something blue, and a sixpence in your shoe. So, you're set, right? Wrong. Here's another whole list of details that may not be fun (and certainly aren't special) but are absolutely necessary for winding up married—and for all those other things you plan on doing afterward. In other words, these are the little things that count.

MARRIAGE LICENSE You and your groom-to-be will need to apply together in person for your marriage license, but before you go traipsing down to the courthouse, call ahead to see what documents are required. Rules for obtaining a marriage license vary from state to state (and county to county), so be sure and check with your county courthouse or the country's U.S. embassy or tourism bureau where you'll be married for proper procedures.

For all marriage licenses, you will need to present an accepted form of identification, such as a passport, driver's license, military ID, or birth certificate. If you have been married before, you will need to present proof of your divorce or a death certificate for your former spouse. All licenses also require a fee, which varies from county to county. Check to see how this fee is payable: cash, check, or money order.

Many states as well as countries also have age and residency requirements. Find out what these are well in advance of the wedding. Also note whether there are any special requirements for you or your groom-to-be if one of you is from a foreign country. Many marriages that are legal in the United States may not necessarily be legal in your or his home country (a fact one bride found out when trying to change her name on her French passport after being married in Michigan).

Wedding Myth # 45: **If you forget your marriage license, your officiant will be happy to perform your ceremony as long as you bring it to him the next day.** *Your officiant will absolutely, positively not perform your ceremony without a marriage license.*

In most states, you will receive your license immediately, but there may be a waiting period after the license is issued before your ceremony can be performed. Be aware that your marriage license may also be valid for a limited amount of time (in most states marriage licenses are valid for sixty days). Also note that if you have already been married in a civil ceremony and are having a minister reaffirm your vows, you will need to bring along a copy of your marriage certificate.

After your officiant has performed the marriage ceremony and signed the certificate, he or she will either return the license to you or mail the license directly to the courthouse. If your officiant returns the license to you, have a family member or your best man or lady swear on his or her life to drop it into the mail for you. Once the signed license is returned to the courthouse, an official marriage certificate will be drawn up with the probate judge's signature and should appear in your mailbox about a month after the wedding.

You may also receive a certificate of marriage from your officiant, which includes your officiant's signature; the signature of two witnesses; and the order of your ceremony, including your vows, scriptures read, and hymns sung. This is a nice memento of your ceremony but may not be considered a legal document.

BLOOD TEST Marriage licenses in many states require a blood test for both you and your groom-to-be. If you live in the same county where the marriage will be performed, your local doctor or county health department can administer a blood test, with results back in two weeks, or for an extra fee, two to three days. Results are good for thirty days from the date the test was administered. If you live outside the state where you will be getting married, your local doctor can administer a blood test—just be sure he runs a check for the state where you will be getting married. Different states check for different types of infections. Your blood test should be signed by the physician who administered the test or by the lab physician who checks the results.

IMMUNIZATION If you are traveling to an exotic country for your wedding or honeymoon, you may need to have your doctor administer an immunization shot for that country's diseases. Call the Centers for Disease Control and Prevention in Atlanta, Georgia (404-332-4559), for information regarding your travel destination or visit their web site at www.cdc.gov.

PRENUPTIAL AGREEMENTS Many brides-to-be and grooms-to-be may want to get a prenuptial agreement. Check with a lawyer for details. These can take awhile to process (and to agree upon), so start negotiations as soon as possible.

CHANGING YOUR NAME If you and/or your groom-to-be will be changing your name after the wedding, you will first need to indicate this on your marriage license application. The courthouse issuing your license will provide you with a Social Security application for changing your name. Applications for changing your name are also available through the Social Security web site at www.ssa.gov or by calling the Social Security general information number at 800-772-1213. You may mail the application in along with proof of your former name (check your application for accepted documents) and proof of your new name (marriage certificate). However, you must send in the original documents and there is no guarantee when these will be returned to you. A better choice is to visit a Social Security office in person. Check your telephone directory under "U.S. Government" listings for the address and telephone number of the office nearest you or call the general 800 number listed above. Your new Social Security card is free and will arrive in approximately two weeks.

After you have changed your name, the next step is to change everything with your name on it, including: driver's license, vehicle registration, voter registration card, passport, employer's records, bank accounts, credit accounts, frequent flyer programs, stocks, bonds, wills, insurance policies, property titles, and medical records. Count on filling out a lot of forms and standing in a lot of lines.

ENGAGEMENT/WEDDING ANNOUNCEMENTS If you would like to run an engagement and/or wedding announcement in your local newspaper, check with the paper for their specific rules. For most publications, there is no fee, but there may also be no guarantee that your announcement will be printed. Most publications require that you fill out a form and most have deadlines for both engagement announcements (often two to six months before the wedding) and wedding announcements (from six weeks to two months after the ceremony). You may also want to run a photograph with your announcement, but be aware that these may not be returned.

PASSPORTS/VISAS If you are traveling out of the country for your wedding or honeymoon, you may need a passport or a visa (if you already have a passport, be sure to check its expiration date). Canada, Mexico, and parts of the Caribbean will accept a birth certificate and photo ID as identification, but be sure and check with your travel agent or the country's board of tourism. You may also need a tourist card, which airlines will either give you on the plane or sell to you at the airport. Some countries also have special requirements for driving. Travel guides, along with many countries' tourism boards' web sites, list all of these requirements.

Passport applications are available at many U.S. post offices, federal courthouses, county clerks' offices, federal buildings, or other government centers. Check your telephone directory for listings under "U.S. Government, Passport" for the office nearest you or call the Federal Information Center at 800-688-9889. To apply for a passport, you will need to bring your application as well as proof of U.S. citizenship; proof of identity containing your signature and physical description or photograph, such as a driver's license; and two identical passport photographs taken within six months of the date of your application. The fee for a passport is $65. Check with your local government office to see how this fee should be paid.

*Wedding Myth #46: **It is quick and easy to get a passport.** It can take up to three months for your passports to arrive, so make sure you apply well in advance of your travel date. Expedited service is available only for early departure, generally with proof of travel and an additional fee.*

Some countries may require a tourist visa as well as a passport, especially if you are staying for an extended period of time. Ask your airline or travel agent about visa requirements as soon as you make your travel plans. To apply for a visa, contact that country's consulate for proper procedures as well as the length of time it takes to get one.

CHECKS/MONEY ORDERS/CERTIFIED CHECKS/CASH The funny thing about most wedding details is that they all need to be paid for. Marriage licenses, blood tests, passports, caterers, florists, photographers—all of these require money. Find out well in advance how this money needs to be paid, and be sure and set aside a day the week before your wedding to withdraw cash and purchase all certified checks and money orders. Most banks are closed on weekends and those that are open are probably at least two hours from your reception site. I, of course, had to discover this the day of my wedding when I sent my dad and uncle out for our band's certified check. Also be sure and have enough personal checks and/or cash on hand the day of your wedding for paying vendors and tipping waiters and bartenders. You might also want to appoint a friend or family member to take care of all the checks and cash for you, since dancing to your band is going to seem like a lot more fun than paying them on your wedding day.

Wedding Countdown

KEEPING TRACK OF THE DETAILS

Details and more details. Now, the trouble with all of these details is that you are going to need to find some way to keep track of them. Here's a tip: Mental notes do not work. I don't care if you are really, really smart and have a very, very large brain. Your brain will not be working two weeks before your wedding. It's one of those unspoken wedding rules that nobody bothers to tell you about. So, I'm telling you: Two weeks before your wedding you are going to be so busy juggling details, fielding phone calls, and taking care of last-minute emergencies that you may very well feel like you're losing your mind. Unfortunately, it seems the details, phone calls, and last-minute problem-solving are actually what ensure that you wind up married. This, of course, still leaves us with the subject of how to keep track of the details. As with your original wedding plan, there are various ways to keep yourself organized. Palm Pilots. Computers. Consultants. One bride, looking for something easy to carry but hard to lose, wrote her to-do lists on the back of her hand each day.

I myself am still a fan of a good old pencil and pad of paper. The weeks before my wedding, I carried a notebook with me at all times, jotting down each detail I needed to take care of, checking it off when I'd finished, and adding new ones as they arose. My mother and I also placed to-do lists on the refrigerator for each member of the family. People could view their tasks and cross them off when completed.

However, creating to-do lists is one thing; organizing to-do lists is something else entirely. Months after the wedding I am still finding slips of paper in books, notebooks, suitcases, and pockets. My mom found a to-do list just the other day in the glove compartment of her car. No wonder, then, that the days before my wedding I felt as if I were going insane.

Wedding Myth #47: **You will not have any last-minute errands to run.** *If you are having a small wedding or hire a wedding coordinator, you may not. If you are having a large wedding and don't hire a wedding coordinator, count on it.*

What is far more helpful is to do a little bit of planning before the actual countdown begins. Sit down with a piece of paper and make a list of absolutely every task you'll need to accomplish before your wedding day. These include all the details that make your wedding special: favors, wedding programs, place cards, as well as the details that aren't so special but are just as important: blood tests, marriage license, your band's outdoor music permit. Assign each task to a specific day, grouping together errands that can be run on the same side of town, faxes that can be sent at the same time, and phone calls you can make all at once. You should also never hesitate to ask for help. Even if friends and family members are working, they may be able to run an errand that's near their office on their lunch break or help with a project—putting together wedding programs, for instance—in the evening or on a weekend. Taking care of the details is always a lot more fun when you have a little company.

Most important, schedule time for yourself. Planning a wedding can seem like a full-time job, and even the most organized bride is apt to feel a bit frenzied. But let's not forget that being a bride is also supposed to be fun. So leave time for eating, relaxing, exercising, and enjoying the company of all the people who have traveled so far to be with you on this special day. Come time for your wedding, you and your groom are going to want to stand in front of your guests glowing from the excitement of the day rather than fainting from all the work it took to get there.

So what does a bride's to-do list look like? What should *yours* look like? What if you can't remember what to put on the to-do list? And how will you manage to actually do everything on the to-do list? Just in case you've lost all hope of ever becoming organized, I've put all my little slips of paper together for you. They include all the things I planned for, as well as a few things I didn't. And while these to-do lists (when I could find them) were at times minor annoyances, when compiled, they tell a much larger and major story: the story of my wedding, complete with all the last-minute wedding details, when I took care of them, who helped me, and why they were all really worth it in the end. So don't despair. I survived. You will, too. Welcome to my ten-day wedding countdown.

DAY NUMBER 1

- Wake up, eat breakfast, and go for a run.

- Get blood test.

- Order bridesmaids' shoes and Mom's shoes from bridal shop.

- Go with Mom to buy tablecloths and napkins for family barbecue on Thursday.

- Visit seamstress for final rehearsal dinner– and wedding-dress alterations.

- Go to final hair appointment, wind up bald, make another hair appointment.

- Go out to eat with my parents, read, and go to bed.

DAY NUMBER 2

- Wake up, eat breakfast, and go for a run.

- Fax band directions to reception site, preferred song list, outfit suggestions, and call to find out about final payment.

- Fax photographer directions to church and rules for indoor photography, and call to confirm makeup appointment for wedding day.

- Call rehearsal-dinner manager with final head count.

- Call reception caterer with final head count.

- Call Brian to remind him to pick up wedding rings at jeweler.

- Eat dinner with my parents, read, and go to bed.

DAY NUMBER 3

- Wake up, eat breakfast, and go for a run.

- Call florist to confirm flower selections and order arrangements for Brian's mother's and stepmother's hotel rooms.

- Call church secretary and wedding director to confirm rehearsal time and minister to confirm order of ceremony.

- Call to confirm honeymoon reservations.

- Call to order reception favors.

- Spend two and a half hours with Mom at hairstylist getting hair extensions put in.

- Spend four and a half hours with Mom in bathroom at home taking them out.

- Call friend to cancel plans because I cannot possibly be seen in public.

- Eat dinner with my parents, contemplate reading, and go to bed.

DAY NUMBER 4

- Wake up, eat breakfast, and go for a run.

- Pick up aunt at airport.

- Finish out-of-town guests' schedules for their hotel rooms so they will know where to be, when to be there, and how to get there.

- Finish sorting through baby pictures of Brian and me to put on tables during rehearsal dinner.

- Finish making place cards and seating chart for rehearsal dinner.

- Finish printing and copying wedding programs and tie each of the 200 together with ribbons.

- Eat dinner with parents and aunt, read, and go to bed.

DAY NUMBER 5

- Wake up, eat breakfast, and go for a run.

- Read newspaper. Lie in sun.

- Go with Mom to pick up rehearsal-dinner and wedding dresses.

- Drop off dry cleaning.

- Stop at Pilar's house and meet her dogs.

- Stop by fruit and vegetable stand and pick out fruit and vegetables.

- Eat fruit and vegetables with parents and aunt, read, and go to bed.

DAY NUMBER 6

- Wake up, eat breakfast, and go for a run.

- Call caterer to confirm they have generator for band.

- Find out caterer does not have generator for band.

- Call band to find out what kind of generator they need.

- Call rental company to rent generator.

- Find out band didn't really know what kind of generator they needed.

- Call local music store to find out what kind of generator band will need.

- Call rental company and rent generator.

- Eat dinner with parents, aunts, and cousins, and go to bed.

DAY NUMBER 7

+ Wake up, eat breakfast, and go for a run.

+ Pick up blood test results.

+ Pick up dry cleaning.

+ Pick up favors for reception.

+ Take cousins to buy shirts, pants, and ties for the wedding. Try to explain why ties are necessary.

+ Eat dinner with parents, aunt, and Brian, who has just arrived from New York, and go to bed.

DAY NUMBER 8

+ Wake up, eat breakfast, and skip run.

+ Deliver out-of-town guests' wedding schedules to hotel.

+ Pick up Brian and get marriage license.

+ Have Brian and cousin buy alcohol for reception, deliver alcohol to caterer, pick up trophies for golf tournament, and apply for outdoor music permit for band. (Note: Three days before the wedding was plenty of time in Athens, Georgia, to apply for a music permit. If your wedding is in a larger city, you may need to leave more time.)

+ Call best friend and ask her if she will pick up bridesmaids' shoes and Mom's shoes from bridal shop and bring them to the brunch the next morning.

- Observe with mild shock as my mom and cousin make coleslaw, potato salad, fruit salad, mixed bean salad, corn on the cob, baked beans, and strawberry shortcake for the BBQ.

- Everybody arrives for BBQ.

- Eat a lot of food and go to bed.

DAY NUMBER 9

- Wake up, eat breakfast, and go for a run.

- Pack the car with bridesmaids' dresses, bridesmaids' hose, place cards, pictures for the rehearsal dinner, and the cereal, bib, and bag that were left at the barbecue.

- Arrive at the brunch. Eat a little bit of food and drink a lot of margaritas.

- Have bridesmaids take place cards and pictures to the rehearsal dinner restaurant.

- Go with Mom to final hair appointment.

- Attend ceremony rehearsal.

- Attend rehearsal dinner.

- Laugh, eat, drink, kiss Brian good night, and go to bed.

DAY NUMBER 10: WEDDING DAY!

- Wake up, take long bath, and eat breakfast. Too nervous to run.

- Send Dad and uncle on a two-hour drive to the only bank open on a Saturday to get certified check for band.

- Have nails done.

- Pack up dress, all other wedding paraphernalia, and marriage license.

- Meet hairstylist and makeup artist at church for hair and makeup appointments.

- Greet friends and family as they arrive to help me prepare for big day.

- Pay florist, photographer, minister, organist, violinist, and wedding director.

- Put on wedding dress.

- Have pictures taken with bridesmaids and my family.

- Eat a cookie.

- Go to the bathroom.

- Watch everyone leave for church sanctuary.

- Hug my dad as he puts my veil over my face and the most beautiful, wonderful day of my life begins.

There are no more details after this. Well, there are, but you will immediately forget all about them. Even if you happen to remember one or two, you will almost certainly forget why in the world they were ever important. After all, the most beautiful, wonderful day of your life has just begun.

PART IV

During

The Rehearsal

IF AT FIRST YOU DON'T SUCCEED,
TRY, TRY AGAIN

You've made all of the wedding plans, confirmed all of the wedding plans; now, forget all of the wedding plans. Huh? Yep, just throw them all to the wind. For the past months you've been busy (okay, bonkers) finding a dress, returning the shoes, hiring a photographer, firing a caterer, choosing a florist, and booking a band among many, many other things. Now, if you're not careful, your wedding may wind up simply feeling like a relief rather than the grand occasion you've always dreamed of. Hint: The weekend of your wedding, relax. Breathe. Enjoy. Starting with your wedding rehearsal.

If you are having a ceremony that involves more than, oh, five people, you may need to have a rehearsal. A rehearsal involves umpteen things you will be thinking about for the very first time, including: lining up bridesmaids and groomsmen, processing and recessing them down an aisle, deciding on an order for seating the mothers and grandmothers, assigning an usher or groomsmen for each one, deciding when to lift the bride's veil, agreeing on how her parents should present her, and, well, a dozen other things we'll get to in a bit.

Processing and recessing and lighting candles may sound rather easy to you now, but amid meeting and greeting friends and family, people have a tendency to forget how to do simple things like walk and talk and stand and, most important, listen. Listening, I have learned, is one of the first skills to go, which is why you will want to arrange for a super-duper wedding director with a loud, commanding voice who will make people listen whether they want to or not. Now, your wedding party and family may be a docile bunch with nothing more on their minds than lining up on church steps and processing slowly down the aisle. Or, your wedding party may be of the type more interested in back-slapping and flicking boogers on each other's lapels. I won't tell you which category my wedding party fell into. I'll just say I was glad to have Terre, instead of me, telling folks what to do. Besides, a wedding director has directed many, many weddings before yours and will know the best way to keep things moving quickly and smoothly.

*Wedding Myth #48: **The wedding party will be on time to the rehearsal.** Perhaps. Just in case, build in an extra half-hour or so to account for friends and family who will get lost, stuck in traffic, or who can never seem to remember to wear a watch.*

Many houses of worship with rules regarding ceremonies have a list of wedding directors from which you can choose. Their services may cost a small fee but are necessary and worth every single penny. If you are having an outdoor ceremony or a ceremony at a location that does not provide a coordinator, you will still need to find someone to direct your ceremony. The following story (courtesy of my best friend) demonstrates why.

"I was recently at a wedding where none of the bridesmaids had ever been in a wedding before. Although someone had a vague idea that they were supposed to walk down the aisle, nobody knew exactly how this was supposed to occur. I ended up having to take charge and line the bridesmaids and groomsmen up and cue them when to walk down the aisle or walk in from the side of the altar with the groom. Unfortunately, because the chapel was all glass, the day of the wedding there wasn't anywhere for the girls or guys—or even the bride and groom—

to hide from the guests. And nobody was in the church to hear the organ music so nobody knew when to walk in. Everything was completely out of control."

To make sure your "I dos" go smoothly, find, hire, or appoint a wedding director. You may have a perfectly capable friend (Betsy, for instance, has been in round about eight weddings and can direct a ceremony in her sleep). I have also seen a bossy mother work effectively. In any case, you will also want to make sure this person is present the day of your wedding to tell everybody all over again what to do since most people will have completely forgotten.

Most important, your wedding rehearsal will give your officiant the opportunity to go through the ceremony with both you and your groom-to-be as well as with the wedding party and your families. Our minister began the rehearsal with a prayer, a wonderful way for everyone to pause, catch their breaths, and reflect on the reasons we were all gathered together in the first place. He explained the meanings behind each aspect of the ceremony, reminding Brian and me of what our marriage symbolized and introducing the wedding party to my faith's particular beliefs. We practiced when to step up to the altar (my sister's cue to straighten my veil and take my bouquet), when to take each other's hands, when to say our vows, when to exchange rings, when to light the unity candle, when to kneel, and when to face the congregation as husband and wife (another veil-straightening here).

During the rehearsal, family members and friends participating in the ceremony will have the opportunity to practice their readings and solos and should be given their appropriate cues to begin. Make sure all microphones and lights are working. (A friend of mine attended a wedding during which the church suddenly went black. A nest of squirrels had apparently eaten through the electrical wires in the attic.) Your organist or musicians may also want to be present to practice the processional and recessional music in tandem with the wedding party. Purcell's "Trumpet Voluntary" may need to last five minutes or five seconds depending on how many bridesmaids you have tripping down the aisle. This will also give your mother the opportunity to bawl her eyes out during "Sunrise, Sunset" before the actual ceremony. (Brian's very thoughtful groomsmen brought along tissues for just such an occasion.)

Your rehearsal also marks the moment when all of your planning is done and the wedding itself is about to begin. It may also be one of the first—and last—opportunities that you and your groom-to-be have to see each other away from the vying attentions of families and friends. If you can arrange it, arrive at your ceremony site a little bit before the rest of the wedding party. An empty church, synagogue, or banquet hall is often the perfect place to enjoy a bit of peace and quiet. Even just a quick, silent kiss may be enough to calm your racing hearts and churning stomachs and fill them instead with the gentlest of flutters and the lightest of butterfly wings.

The Rehearsal Dinner

TOASTS, JOKES, AND OTHER
EMBARRASSING MOMENTS

While you are busy contemplating those flutters in your heart and butterflies in your stomach, let me share with you my latest epiphany: Weddings are the modern-day equivalent of Greek and Roman dramas. *Huh?* Now, before you decide I've gone completely mad, bear with me. This is interesting stuff and also very relevant to your understanding of what a rehearsal dinner is all about, so pay attention.

These dramas, staged for the public over the course of three days (sound familiar?), came in two types: tragedies and comedies. In the tragedies, there was much moaning and groaning and weeping and tearing of hair. In fact, actors were often left bald at the end of a performance (uncanny, isn't it?). The elements (earth, wind, fire, and water) often made spectacular appearances, which resulted in complete mayhem. These plays, however, were not to be taken literally. All physical activities were merely outward expressions of inward, spiritual, transformations. Through the power of love, the hero and heroine were often able to not necessarily avert the tragedy, but to somehow transcend it. In other words, love triumphed over all. And to help out the audience, there was almost always a chorus, a vehicle for the common man to cheer, jeer, share histories and traditions, tell tales short and tall, and in any number of ways, embarrass (or aid, depending on their disposition) the hero and heroine.

Welcome to your rehearsal dinner: a chorus of family and friends who will cheer, jeer, share histories and traditions, tell tales short and tall, and in any number of ways, attempt to embarrass or aid you and your handsome groom-to-be. Now, choruses come in many shapes and sizes. Anika and Mike's, for example, consisted of all of her closest friends and family, some of whom had flown all the way from Norway. During an intimate dinner at Anika's family's country club, Anika's aunt and uncle stood up and demonstrated the proper way for a wife to beat her husband over the head with a rolling pin. The story goes that in Norwegian households, it is the husband's duty to tell his wife what to do. This being the case, the wife is obviously going to need a rolling pin. Before Anika received her rolling pin, however, all of her wedding guests were asked to sign it. Anika was then instructed that before she was allowed to actually beat Mike up side the head, she must first sit down with him and read all of the wedding guests' signatures and wishes for a happy marriage. The hope was that by the time they were done, Anika wouldn't still feel like hitting him. A nice tradition for a chorus to share (obviously meant to aid the lucky couple) and a very tender introduction to marriage if I do say so myself.

> **Wedding Myth # 49: *Your best man will automatically know how to give a toast.*** *No best man really knows how to give a toast. Unfortunately, you are not allowed to tell him. Fortunately, your groom is.*

At our own rehearsal dinner, Brian and I decided to share our histories through pictures. We sorted through old and new photographs of us and our families and friends, made color copies, and had them inserted in each table's arrangement of red and white peonies. This was a wonderful way for families and friends who didn't know each other to share stories, and as it turned out, to learn rather embarrassing things about us, the lucky (or unlucky) couple. At Nelly's rehearsal dinner, her stepfather prepared a similar treat for guests—a surprise slide show documenting her and her fiancé's significant life moments. It was a delightful way for their families to meet and a touching tribute to the bride and groom and their accomplishments.

Many brides and grooms choose to have toasts given at their wedding receptions instead of at the rehearsal dinner. The best man or perhaps the bride's father offers the first toast and is followed by whoever happens to be closest to the microphone. For smaller receptions, this may be appropriate. However, be aware that at larger receptions, these speeches tend to grow to epic lengths (borrowing from the Greeks again), and really, why hire a band if you're not going to get to hear it? In fact, you may want to instruct your bandleader to tell guests that, at the bride and groom's request, toasts will be made only by the father of the bride, the best man, and the best lady. Rehearsal dinners are by far a better place to reminisce about days of old, where only your closest family and friends will be present to hear what you may prefer your boss and coworkers didn't. Some family stories were meant to remain family stories.

Wedding Myth #50: Your dad will automatically know how to give a toast. No dad really knows how to give a toast. This is okay as long as his toast is shorter and less embarrassing than the best man's.

Swirling around this whole chorus of events, of course, will be the drama itself. Sometimes, unfortunately, the drama could wind up being tragic. Dorie, for instance, arrived at the rehearsal dinner (hosted by her groom's parents) to discover that the groom's side consisted of about thirty people, while she had been allowed to invite only ten guests. Even more insulting was the fact that the waiters, well aware of who was footing the bill, completely ignored the bride's family. Much fighting ensued between families, friends, and even the bride and groom.

Becca's rehearsal dinner was equally as tumultuous. For starters, the groom's mother and father were in the same room for the first time in twenty years. Cocktails flowed steadily to ease the tension. Meanwhile, Becca's own family was having a meltdown of their own. Should her stepfather walk her down the aisle? Her real father? Or both her real father and mother? Completely confused, Becca ran off to hide in the bathroom only to discover the groom's mother throwing up in one of the stalls.

Most of the tragic rehearsal dinner stories I've heard involve problems between families. His mother doesn't like your mother. Your mother doesn't like his. Your mother-in-law doesn't like you. If you know this is the case ahead of time, you may want to try and keep family members on opposite sides of the room. Have friends and family keep the feuding factions occupied. Food, drink, conversation, perhaps one more drink have been known to do the trick. Or, you may want to nix the idea of a group dinner entirely. Spend a quiet dinner with your family while your groom spends one with his, and then meet up later with friends and out-of-town guests.

> *Wedding Myth* # 51: **Moms can't give toasts.** *Moms toasts are always the best. For one thing, they actually sound sincere when quoting Shakespeare or Elizabeth Barrett Browning.*

All rehearsal dinners, however, whether tragic or comic, are great practice. For, in the end, that is exactly what a rehearsal dinner is all about: rehearsal. Think of yours as one big practice wedding, full of tragedies and comedies, floods and fights, toasts and jokes, and with each event, shrug off another worry, another one of those last-minute, what-if wedding woes, until there are none left and you, your groom-to-be, and the rest of the chorus are having a good time. By the way, the audiences attending those dramas came because they were fun. Even during the tragedies, they knew that eventually, love would triumph over all.

The Ceremony

I DO (I THINK)

Moments before her ceremony, Jamie was hyperventilating into a paper bag. Jacque, in full dress, makeup, and hair, was sitting in her car in the parking lot honking the horn and screaming at the absolute top of her lungs. Ann's nerves struck the night before her ceremony when she threw the phone out of her apartment window, certain she was never going to talk to Duncan again, much less marry him. And then there was Jennifer, who, the morning of her wedding, decided to go skydiving.

Now, "taking the plunge" (as in your ceremony) can be nerve-racking. You've finished the planning, taken care of all of the details; you're even prepared in case of an emergency. There's really nothing left to do now but go through with the whole thing. And that can induce a serious case of the wedding-day jitters. In only the most extreme cases, however, should you take these as a sign you're about to make the mistake of a lifetime. What is far more likely is that your body, which has physically and mentally been going at about ninety miles an hour for the last week or so, is suddenly in shock at being, well, *still*. Those hours before your ceremony, having your makeup done, your hair put up, your dress put on can be rather slow. And quiet. Unfortunately, nobody has bothered to warn your mind about this, and it's still racing. All sorts of wacky one-syllable words are likely to pop into your head: Huh? What? When? Why? But. Oh. My. God. Aaaaaagh.

Or, you might discover you're a bride-to-be like me whose brain simply decided to stop working altogether. At the first hint that it was no longer needed, my mind went completely blank. I wasn't frantic. I wasn't worried. I wasn't breathing heavily or shouting out loud or doing anything at all that required energy. I simply watched as all of my closest family and friends gathered together in the parlor of my church to help me get ready. People tied ribbons on programs, played CDs, picked out songs on the piano, and talked about the festivities the night before (which was nice since some of the details were already a little foggy).

The storm was over. The wedding was finally here. I was calm and happy and extremely, extremely quiet. I couldn't think of the first thing to say to people besides "I'm getting married," which, of course, was already pretty evident and made me look a little foolish. But I wasn't worried. I smiled like crazy for the photographs of all the bridesmaids and me and smiled even more crazily for the pictures with my family. I wasn't throwing telephones, but I was certainly a little loony, which meant, according to the mysterious rules of weddings, I was ready. A good thing, because not long after I had this thought, our wedding director came to get me and my dad and announced what I had been waiting a very long time to hear: "It's time."

> *Wedding Myth* #52: **This is your wedding day—nothing can go wrong.** *Of course it can. Sue walked into her chapel and discovered an open casket at the altar (the chapel director had scheduled a funeral at the exact same time as her wedding). Missing grooms, fainting brides, late ministers, fighting groomsmen. These are called catastrophes. As long as you wind up married, none of them matter.*

And the wedding ceremony? It was beautiful: the sunlight streaming in through the church's stained-glass windows, the white hydrangeas with tiny tendrils of green on either side of the altar, the shining unity candle, the wedding party, the wedding guests, our families, the hymns, the readings, my dress. And although I couldn't see it, I was sure what was left of the hair on my head looked beautiful, too.

But do you know what was even more beautiful? Brian. My exquisitely beautiful brown-eyed boy and the moment we shared in front of the altar exchanging vows. And it had absolutely nothing to do with the stained-glass windows or the flowers or the dress or my hair. It had nothing to do with the programs and their ribbons or the schedules that finally got copied or the favors we accidentally left at home. Sure, the details counted. Sure, they made our wedding special. But nothing, nothing was as special as those moments standing in front of the altar as we joined our lives together.

"I now pronounce you husband and wife. . . . You may kiss the bride."

Wow! Let the bells peal! Let us recess, let us process again, let us do anything in the world! We're married! Nothing else matters!

If these thoughts sound familiar, it's because they're the very same ones you had just after you got engaged. And, oddly enough, the very same things happen next: You smile a lot, you kiss a lot, you hold hands a lot, you, well, turn to the next chapter.

The Reception

WHERE'S THE PARTY?

So what else do you do right after your ceremony? You celebrate! Coincidentally, right after this most spectacular of events, there is a huge party, or a brunch, or a lunch, or a breakfast, or a tea, or a dessert to celebrate with. Weddings may be a little wacky and there are a million things wrong with them, but they do manage to get some things completely right. Of course, there may be a few things to take care of before you actually head off to the party—like photographs and receiving lines—but again, none of it really matters. If you thought you were a little loony before the ceremony, just wait until afterward. There's something about gazing into another person's eyes that intensely for that long that makes a person slightly loopy (Sarah described it as a little like watching yourself in a dream, and Amy was convinced her head was floating around like a balloon).

So believe me, no matter what's going on after those "I dos," none of it is going to matter much. Take my reception, for instance. After a few photos at the church with Brian and our families, we were whisked away to the Taylor-Grady House, a beautifully restored Greek revival home built in the 1840s. Tables and chairs had been set on the porch, wicker chairs had been set across the lawn, and guests were milling around everywhere.

Buffet tables and a bar had been laid out under the trees, and under the tent was the main buffet, a mouth-watering spread of grilled fresh hams with apple barbecue sauce and sweet potato biscuits, baked garlic cheese grits with tomato pudding, grilled and marinated boneless chicken breasts with peach salsa, and an endless number of other delectable Southern treats. Tables under the tent had been draped with white tablecloths and decorated with floating candles and rose petals. Rose petals had even been scattered across the entire front porch, providing a soft red-and-white carpet for guests to prance on.

Our cake, a spectacular white creation with deep-red rose petals arranged around each layer, sat majestically inside the house, where guests were oohing and aahing and laughing over the surprise groom's cake—a not quite so-perfect replica of Brian's favorite game, Flick-A-Nik. In an adjoining room, another bar served cocktails as well as fresh-squeezed lemonade, and a large dining room table was laden with even more food. Roses, in every color, were everywhere. And in the exact middle of the house was the grand oak staircase where Brian and I descended for the first time as husband and wife. It was all more beautiful than I ever could have imagined, and for a moment (or two) I found myself a bit overwhelmed.

Then, my sister ran to find a pair of scissors, we cut off the bottom of my veil, and I was off, with Brian in tow, to meet and greet and dance and drink and celebrate. After all, that's what we were there to do. Brian and I danced our first dance to the band's rendition of Frank and Nancy Sinatra's "Somethin' Stupid," and then Brian and his mother and my dad and I swayed tearily to "You've Got a Friend." For the third dance of the evening, the groomsmen seized Brian and me and perched us atop their shoulders. I laughed, screamed, and managed—barely— to keep my veil attached to my head. Brian shoved cake in my face (yes, he did). I stabbed him with the knife (no, I didn't). And my dad and Brian's oldest brother made rousing, even reckless, toasts to us, the very lucky couple (copies are available upon request). I threw the bouquet. Tina caught it. And then Brian and I were running back down that red-brick path amid the glittering lights of a hundred or so sparklers.

Oh, it was beautiful. And were there problems? Of course, it was a wedding, and it wouldn't be a wedding without something going wrong. We left at home all the folding fans we had bought for guests. A portion of our wine and champagne didn't arrive. The buffet tablecloths were not exactly what we had ordered. For a while, the band was so loud guests had to take refuge inside the house. And because we hadn't managed to hire a coordinator for the day, there was slight confusion over when to have the first dance, when to slice the cake, and when in the world to toss the bouquet. What did we do? We arranged for someone else to take care of the problems and relied on our most excellent photographer to cue us when it was time to make our entrance and exit and, if I do say so myself, our exquisitely executed first dance.

> *Wedding Myth* #53: **This is your wedding day—the weather will be perfect.** *Right in the middle of Dana's outdoor reception, a thunderstorm struck. The tent leaked. The band packed up and went home. All of the guests' shoes got muddy. So, everyone took off their shoes, went inside, and turned on the stereo. As long as you're married, does the weather really matter?*

Yes, there will be some accidents—some problems, some mishaps, emergencies of one kind or another. But here's a little hint: Whatever happens—for better or for worse—you are alive, you are in love, and you are married. So relax, do a shot, sip some sake, sip some tea, do the shag, do the shimmy, do the shuffle, do the shake, have a smoke, have a smell of your flowers, have some challah bread, sing a song, slip in a kiss, share a dance, share some dessert. It's your day, your wedding—do absolutely anything, anything in the world you want to do. Because, hey (repeat with me): You're married—nothing else matters!

Wait, surely some things matter. I mean, my reception is a big affair. Or it's a small affair but it's a big deal. Surely there must be some rules. Surely you can give us a little advice. Oh, if you insist.

RECEPTION RULES TO REMEMBER

1. HOLD HANDS. As soon as you arrive at your reception, grab your groom's hand and hold on tight. There are going to be a ton of other people grabbing your hand (and his), and for this one day, you really don't want to be separated. Mixing and mingling hand in hand is far more enjoyable than trying to catch a glimpse of your groom over a sea of 150 guests. I mean, you just married the dear boy, don't you want to hold on to him?

2. HUDDLE. Right after you've grabbed your groom's hand, grab the hands of your best man and best lady and head for your wedding director, caterer, or headwaiter. Make sure everything is running smoothly, answer any last-minute questions, and direct whoever is putting this grand affair together to let your best man or lady know if there are any problems. That way, you can continue to smile like the loons you are and dance and eat and drink and laugh without a care in the world. You will also want to have a personal huddle with your best man and lady to let them know any requests you may have, such as, "A glass of champagne would be absolutely delightful," or "Please tell that DJ to stop playing the macarena before I break both of his thumbs." Your best man and lady will do whatever you want, whenever you want it, wherever they happen to be, just to make sure you are having the absolute best time ever. That's what best men and ladies do.

3. HAVE FUN. Above all, have fun. You've worked hard to get here. Now it's time to relax. That means no hissy fits, no hollering, no hullabaloos, and certainly no horrible, hateful behavior. This is a wedding, and while accidents will happen, accusing others of causing them shouldn't. I mean, what would you have to talk about if everything went according to plan? Plus, we threw all those plans out the window a long time ago. Now it's time to parrteeeeee!

4. HIRE A WEDDING-DAY COORDINATOR. Okay, this is actually something you are supposed to do before the reception, but some brides-to-be get so caught up in the rest of the details they may forget this one. Don't forget this one. It may sound silly now, but the day of your reception, with all of those stars in your eyes and bells in your ears, you are never going to remember when to have the first dance, when to slice the cake, when to begin toasts, or when to do anything other than smile like a couple of goofballs. To keep the day running smoothly, hire someone to take care of the details for you. Your coordinator should arrive at the same time as your vendors to make sure everyone and everything is in their appropriate places and to answer questions and take care of any and all emergencies. Some reception sites will provide a coordinator for you. If yours doesn't, many wedding planners offer their services for a day (although some may insist on planning the whole affair). The important point is to have someone to keep an eye on the time (because you certainly won't) and to keep the reception humming along. After all, you and your groom are here to celebrate, not coordinate.

5. HIDE OUT. Oh, not for the whole ceremony. Just for a few minutes or so. At Jewish weddings, the bride and groom are ushered into a side room somewhere to enjoy a moment to themselves before returning to the reception, relaxed and ready to meet and greet guests. The bride should also have a moment to herself, too. At some point during the reception, slip into a side garden, or to the side of the dance floor, and take it all in. Watch your mother laughing with your great-aunt. Watch your dad preparing for his toast. Watch your groom's parents swinging the flower girl around the dance floor. And watch your groom desperately searching for you. The day is going to be over before you know it. Take a breath and etch in your memory this perfect vision of a perfect day (and hurry up, because your groom is heading your way).

6. HELLO. All of your guests deserve a great big "hello" from both you and your groom. Whether you greet them in a receiving line or walk around to each guest during the reception, you should take the oppor-

tunity to talk with everyone. Some couples may decide to let guests come up to them—just be certain your guests are comfortable doing this. Brides and grooms often appear so busy, guests may feel awkward interrupting. And would you really want someone to go home without having a chance to congratulate you? Your guests have taken time out of their days to attend this special event—make sure you take the time to thank them.

7. HAVE A DOGGY BAG MADE TO GO. If you are having a buffet dinner reception, know from the very start that you are not going to get to eat a single bite. You will not sit down. You will not eat. You may or may not drink. You will, however, be smiling for photographs, talking to guests, kissing your aunt and uncle and grandmother, perhaps even belting out a special rendition of "Billy Boy" for your guests and groom. In other words, your mouth is going to be so busy it's not going to have a moment to swallow even a morsel of that delectable-looking pâté. And after the reception, your stomach is going to notice. Have your caterer put together a basket of food for you and your groom, including slices of cake and a bottle of wine or champagne. And since your arms are going to be so worn out from performing all those new swing moves, you may also need to arrange for a certain special someone to feed you.

The Getaway

Duck, smile, and run like the wind.

PART V

After

The Honeymoon

GOING, GOING, GONE

So now that you've got a husband, what do you do with him? You go on a honeymoon! What kind of honeymoon? Any kind you want. Nicole and Randy spent a month sailing around the islands of Greece with their very own boat and captain. Maria and John spent two weeks in a friend's house in Florence, venturing out occasionally for tours of Venice and Rome. Leanne and Andrew spent a weekend at a bed and breakfast on an island off the coast of Seattle. Like weddings, honeymoons come in all shapes and sizes. The most important thing is to take one. Whether you can escape for two weeks, or just two days, celebrating your marriage with an intimate trip for two is one of the most important (oh, okay, awesome) parts of your wedding. It's a once-in-a-lifetime opportunity to spend not necessarily money but time with each other, something you've probably done little of in the last months of planning your wedding, and something you won't get to do again for quite a while once that thing called real life kicks in. In fact, taking a honeymoon is fundamentally about ignoring real life for as long as you possibly can.

Ignoring real life does, however, require a plan. But not to worry. Putting together a honeymoon plan is just like putting together a wedding plan (which you've just done with great success), only a whole lot simpler and a lot more fun.

WHO

Who is your honeymoon for? You and your husband. No family, no friends, and absolutely no children. This is for you and him. Period. (See? I told you this was simple.)

WHAT

Again, you should have absolutely any kind of honeymoon you want. Your wedding day may end with your getaway, but your wedding dream doesn't, so sit down with your honey and discuss just exactly what kind of honeymoon would make you both the happiest newly-weds in the world. Cruising through the Caribbean, skiing in Aspen, museum-hopping through Italy, scuba diving in the Red Sea, golfing across Ireland? Of course, just because your groom would love to spend twelve hours a day on a golf course doesn't mean you would. And just because you'd love to plan a marathon of snorkeling, kayaking, and para-sailing doesn't mean that he would. This is okay. You're married, not joined at the hip. Choose an island where you can join him for a round of golf in the morning and then sail off for an afternoon of snorkeling on your own. Plus, I have a hunch you'll be spending at least a couple of days doing nothing at all (at least not outside the bedroom). A honeymoon is about enjoying yourselves—and each other.

Your honeymoon may also be about trying some exotic new activities you've never even heard of: hippo spotting in Kenya, moose watching in Maine, swimming with the dolphins in Bermuda, or peeking at the pecking parrot fish in your own over-water bungalow in Bora Bora. The opportunities are endless, so take this time to do a little bit of research. Travel magazines, travel books, travel agents, travel web sites—all are great sources of information for choosing a destination, near or far, that matches your personality, his personality, even your budget.

Because honeymoons do require a little something we talked about earlier in the book: money.

My one piece of advice when it comes to this commodity is that if you can, indulge, indulge, indulge. There is nothing quite like pampering yourselves silly on your honeymoon, as Olivia will attest. "Matthew was in charge of planning the honeymoon, and every once in awhile I'd overhear him making arrangements: first-class airplane tickets; the luxury, ocean-view suite; a private sunset sail. At first I was nervous, but then I realized that while the wedding day was my dream, this was his, and he'd been saving accordingly. And while our wedding day was amazing, our honeymoon was even more amazing. Every minute was about spending time together in the most intimate and romantic ways. Finding the person of your dreams to marry is like a little miracle. On your honeymoon, you should celebrate that miracle the very best way you can." Money may not always buy happiness, but it can certainly be fun to try for a week or so.

WHEN

When should you go on your honeymoon? Immediately after your wedding. Although most brides and grooms say it's wise to wait a day before departing (to do laundry, pack, finish unwrapping wedding presents, find your passports), waiting any longer can be anticlimactic.

Sometimes, however, real life doesn't make this easy. Summerlin and Doug, for example, were able to wait until Doug's graduation from law school to hold their wedding, but they only had a few days afterward until he had to take his bar exam. Their solution: a weekend honeymoon at home. "We unplugged the phone, ordered in every night, and burned dozens of candles. We knew we'd eventually get to take a honeymoon, but we also wanted to maintain the romance of our wedding as long as possible." Time and money may be in short supply, but spending a little love can go a long way.

Deciding when to take your honeymoon can also mean considering the weather of your destination. Research the state's or country's average temperatures during the time of year you'll be traveling, as well as possible rainy seasons and popular tourist seasons. Many Caribbean islands, for example, have beautiful weather year-round but only a handful of tourists during October and November. By traveling during an off-peak time you'll enjoy lower rates—and have those beautiful beaches all (or mostly) to yourselves. And although Paris is lovely in the springtime, it can be just as enjoyable in the fall when you won't be fighting crowds through the city's museums. Any European city, however, is a no-no in August, when the locals go on holiday, locking up shops, bakeries, even hotels behind them.

WHERE

Based on what kind of honeymoon you and your husband would like to take and when you'll be traveling, you've probably already started looking at possible destinations. Now's the time to look further. Interested in idling on a Caribbean beach? Choose a specific island. Each one has a distinct personality, from the bistros and boutiques of the French St. Lucia to the astonishing reefs of the Cayman Islands to the rain forests of the Dominican Republic. Or perhaps you have your heart set on an Italian adventure. Consider whether you'd prefer a romp through the ruins of Rome or a cruise through the canals of Venice. Looking to escape the summer heat? Try a tour of Alaska's icebergs or a visit to the blustery shores of Ireland (the perfect time to research your family roots—and stay in a romantic castle).

You should also take this time to start researching where you'd like to stay. An all-inclusive resort, a quaint bed and breakfast, or perhaps simply an eco-friendly campground. Different types of rooms have different types of rates, so make sure you understand exactly what kind of room you'll be staying in and what services the rate includes. Many hotels offer special packages, which include all meals, drinks, and activities during your stay. Or, you may prefer a plan that includes breakfast only, allowing you to dine at different local restaurants at night. If you're taking a cruise, check to see if your room is inside or outside. Inside rooms are less expensive but don't come with a view. Also ask about a potential property's facilities, which may include a pool and a tennis court—or three pools, five tennis courts, a spa, and a golf course. Does the hotel offer room service? Private dinner on the beach? Complimentary champagne? Sometimes simply asking nicely means getting something nice in return.

WHY

You've forgotten already? Because you're married, that's why. And when it comes to honeymoons, there's no reason to rationalize, no room for guilt, and absolutely no need for explanations of any kind. Your family understands. Your friends are envious. And you, my friend, are married. So live it up. Or wind down. Or satisfy your senses by doing a little bit of both. There's only one rule when it comes to honeymoons: enjoy.

HOW

After deciding on what kind of honeymoon you'd like to take, when you'd like to take it, and where you'd like to go—and realizing that it's not really a question of "why" but "why not"—it's time to book your flight (or ship or train or automobile) and hotel (or bed and breakfast or cabin or private villa). In other words, it's time to make those reservations. How? One option is to book your honeymoon through a travel agent. Look for one who specializes in your type of trip (a Caribbean cruise; white-water rafting in Colorado) and has actually been to your destination. They'll be able to suggest quality hotels as well as little-known spots for romantic dining. They may even be familiar enough with the concierge of a hotel to arrange for discounts on any activities you'd like to try during your stay. Travel agents may also be aware of special airline discounts that you're not, or be able to recommend package deals that include hotel, meals, and airfare in one low rate. All travel agents should inform you of the travel requirements of the country you'll be visiting—passports, visas, necessary immunizations—as well as answering any other questions you may have: Is it safe to travel outside the resort? Should we bring our own drinking water? Can I special-order vegetarian meals? Your travel agent will find out the answers, providing you with a detailed itinerary and leaving you to do nothing but enjoy the trip.

Of course, you may be the type to enjoy planning a trip yourself. If you or your groom aren't already overwhelmed with the planning of your wedding, take the time to research discounted airfares and check your destination's board of tourism web site for hotel accommodations, local history, and attractions. Combining your own research with a travel agent's knowledge may be the best idea of all, especially if you'll be traveling to a non-English speaking country. Negotiating rates you don't understand can be difficult. And while glossy photos on the Web can be enticing, you'll want to make sure that the hammock you've been dreaming of is actually between two palm trees on a beach and not two wooden posts by an aboveground swimming pool. Your travel agent is also your link to recourse should something go wrong. Your room isn't exactly up to par? Ask them to help you change. Is your heart set on a sunset sail but the concierge insists they're booked for the week? Ask your travel agent to help fit you in—or even recommend another charter service on the island. Travel agents can promise a hotel more business, which may just get you better service.

Either way you decide to book your honeymoon, make sure to receive all tickets (plane, cruise, train), written confirmation of any car reservations (with all policies regarding gas and mileage), and written confirmation of hotel reservations (with check-in and departure dates, phone and fax numbers, address, and payment requirements). And once you receive all of this very valuable information, keep it somewhere safe—that you'll remember. A file labeled "Honeymoon" worked for us and was soon full of clipped travel articles, brochures, and restaurant recommendations from friends. The file wasn't quite as fat as our "Wedding" file, but it was a lot more fun to sort through.

*Wedding Myth #54: **The honeymoon's over after you fly back home.** The honeymoon's never over—especially if you bring a little bit home with you. Rosie and Bob have a framed photograph of a sunset in Santorini over their mantel. Jackie and Dan brought back a canister of sand from the pink beaches of Bermuda. And Stacia and Will started a travel journal in Alaska that they've kept ever since. The wedding's over—the marriage is just beginning.*

TOP-TEN TIPS FOR THE TRIP

Chances are, the week before your honeymoon you're going to be a little wacky worrying about wedding details, not honeymoon details. The following tips, however, are worth paying attention to, especially if you'll be traveling abroad. They guarantee that you and your husband will get to where you're going, enjoy your visit once you do, and happily (or unhappily, depending on how much fun you're having) see that you get back again.

1. Photocopy the first page of your passport (or driver's license) and carry separately from your real passport.

2. Photocopy all prescriptions for medicine and eyeglasses (also be sure to pack extra contact lenses or a second pair of glasses).

3. Photocopy all credit cards in case they're lost or stolen, and write down the numbers of all traveler's checks.

4. Travel with $100 in foreign currency, traveler's checks, and a credit card. If you plan on using a cash card, check with your bank to make sure your PIN number will work overseas.

5. Check to see if you'll need a converter for hair dryers and other small appliances.

6. Take your address book (for contacting friends and family in case of an emergency—and for addressing postcards). Make sure your friends and family have your number and address as well.

7. Just in case, pack a pocket flashlight, extra batteries, extra film, an extra asthma inhaler, Imodium, and a Swiss Army knife.

8. If you'll be doing a lot of walking, include a good pair of walking shoes.

9. If you'll be doing a lot of walking with your luggage, pack lightly.

10. And most important, take a journal, for recording all of those wonderful things that are about to happen next.

WHAT HAPPENS NEXT

Hey, there are *some* things best friends don't talk about.

Acknowledgments

If I've learned absolutely anything over the past year it's that weddings and books do not happen alone. Thank you from the bottom of my heart to everyone who helped me with both. My best friends and wedding party: Anika, Betsy, Beverly, Bob, Emily, Frank, Jennifer, Jeremy, Jessica, John, Kevin C., Kevin L., Laura, Melanie, Mike, Ryan, Sarah, and Shannon. Our wedding choreographers: Shoshana Aron and Le Show Bridal Designs, Athens First United Methodist Church, Martha Braswell, Bill Britt, Ron De Summa and De Summa & Wexler, Inc., East-West Bistro, Terre Egger, Bill Hartnett, Lee Epting Catering, Gayle Morris and GTM Ltd. Hair Designers, Tammy Nance and Scentiments Floral Design, Sara Page, Reaves Engraving, Inc., The Taylor-Grady House, Total Package, and Marisu Wehrenberg and Dream Keeper Productions. My publisher and editor: Judith Regan and Tia Maggini. My agency: Linda Chester, Gary Jaffe, Joanna Pulcini, and Kelly Smith. My in-laws, for opening both their hearts and homes to me: Elaine, Pete, Bob, and Judy. My parents and sister, the very best family a bride (and writer) could ever, ever ask for. And Brian, husband extraordinaire. You are a dream.

Most especially, the brides and grooms everywhere I talked to, wrote to, lunched with, laughed with, and peppered with more questions than there ever were answers. Thank you for your stories, your advice, your humor, and your incredible insights into what is still probably one of life's wackiest traditions: weddings.

DISCARD
Porter County
Library System

PORTER COUNTY PUBLIC LIBRARY SYSTEM